THE SUCCESSFUL PATH TO FINANCIAL AND PHYSICAL FITNESS

Your Winning Wealth and Health Lifestyle Formula

By

Alka Sharma and

Jennifer Nicole Lee

Published by

Live Limitless Publishing Co.

Email: Publishing@sierrarainge.com

www.livelimitlessmedia.com

Jennifer Nicole Lee

Contact Information:

Email: thejennifernicolelee@gmail.com

Website: www.JNLCoaching.com

Printed in the United States of America

Cover Design by: Budi Detikir

Cover Photo by: Joyanne Panton

ISBN:978-1-952903-63-2

Library of Congress Number:

MEDICAL DISCLAIMER

The information is this work is in no way intended as medical advice or as a substitute for medical counseling. This publication contains the opinions and ideas of its Author.

It is intended to provide helpful and informative material on the subjects addressed in the publication. It is sold with the understanding that the author and publisher are not engaged in rendering medical, health, psychological, or any other kind of personal professional services in the book. If the reader requires personal medical, health, or other assistance or advice, a competent professional should be consulted.

The author and publisher specifically disclaim all responsibility for any liability or loss, personal, or otherwise, that is incurred as a consequence, directly or indirectly of the use and application of the contents of this book. Before starting a weight loss plan, a new eating program, or beginning or modifying an exercise program, check with your physician to make sure that the changes are right for you.

"EMPOWER YOUR WEALTH! ENERGIZE YOUR HEALTH!"

Alka Sharma and
Jennifer Nicole Lee

TABLE OF CONTENTS

DEDICATION

To our beloved readers, students, friends, colleagues, fans, believers, and supporters.

As we embark on this journey together through the pages of "The Successful Path to Financial and Physical Fitness: Your Winning Wealth and Health Comprehensive Lifestyle Formula," we extend our deepest gratitude and heartfelt dedication to each and every one of you. It is with immense pride that we stand beside you, knowing that by investing in this book, you are investing in yourselves – in your self-care, self-education, and self-reliance, both financially and physically.

In these pages, we aim to empower you to embrace success as a benchmark of longevity, reminding you that the key to unlocking your fullest potential lies within your commitment to continual learning and growth. Remember, the more you learn, the more you earn, and the more you invest in your financial success alongside your physical well-being, the more enriched and fulfilling your life will become.

We understand the struggles and setbacks that often accompany the pursuit of both financial and physical health. Alka Sharma and Jennifer Nicole Lee, co-authors of this book, have walked that path ourselves – from financial hardship to physical challenges. But we stand before you today as living testaments to the transformative power of resilience, perseverance, and unwavering dedication.

For those of you who may be feeling disheartened or on the brink of giving up, we extend our hands and hearts to you in solidarity. Know that you are not alone in your journey. Let this book be the answer to your prayers, the guiding light that leads you out of the darkness and into a life filled with abundance, vitality, and fulfillment.

So, join us, dear readers, as we embark on this wonderful journey of self-discovery together. With each page turned and each lesson learned, you are one step closer to realizing your financial and physical goals. Together, let us celebrate the beauty of holistic success and the joy of living a truly wonderful life that inspires others to follow suit.

Empower your wealth!
Energize your health!-
Alka Sharma and **Jennifer Nicole Lee**

ACKNOWLEDGEMENTS

We are immensely grateful to our cherished family, loyal clients, supportive colleagues, valued customers, and dedicated fans scattered across the globe. Your unwavering encouragement and belief in our mission propel us forward each day. To our readership, who have embraced our individual projects and now stand with us as we embark on this collective endeavor, we extend our deepest gratitude. Together, we illuminate the path to success in both wealth and health, united in purpose and determination.

A heartfelt acknowledgement is owed to our literary team, Sierra Rainge Jones, the visionary CEO of LIVE LIMITLESS publishing. It is an honor to be included among the esteemed authors under her guidance. We also extend our appreciation to our meticulous editing team, innovative marketing team, and hardworking publicist, whose tireless efforts ensure our message reaches far and wide.

To you, dear reader, holding this book in your hands, we offer our sincerest thanks. Your commitment to self-improvement is commendable, and we are humbled to be a part of your journey. Your feedback and reviews serve as guiding lights, illuminating the path to even greater heights of success and fulfillment.

May the pages within this book serve as a beacon of enlightenment, guiding you towards greater prosperity in both your financial and physical pursuits. We believe wholeheartedly in your potential, and we are excited to witness the extraordinary achievements that lie ahead.

With boundless gratitude and anticipation,
Alka Sharma and **Jennifer Nicole Lee**

OPEN LETTER

Dear Readers,

As authors Alka Sharma and Jennifer Nicole Lee, we stand before you not as mere writers, but as companions on a journey toward a life of abundance in both wealth and health. Our paths have been marked by trials that have tested our resilience, from homelessness to financial instability, and from being out of shape to allowing negative health habits to dominate our lives.

We share our vulnerabilities openly because we have been there. There's no ego in these pages, only a genuine desire to extend a helping hand to those who may find themselves in similar circumstances. We offer solutions born from our own experiences, ones we wish we had known sooner.

In this book, you'll discover actionable strategies to navigate the realms of financial stability and physical fitness with renewed vigor and excitement. Consider it your master plan for self-mastery, designed to unlock the secrets to success in both domains.

But clarity is paramount. We've learned that lack of clarity can lead to undesirable outcomes. That's why we've meticulously outlined plans of action with explicit details, empowering you to become the best version of yourself.

So, how bad do you want it? How fiercely do you desire financial success and physical vitality? Are you willing to train like an athlete, knowing that your life depends on it? Because, in truth, it does.

We embody the ethos of being both business athletes and physical athletes, understanding that true fulfillment lies in mastering both realms. You don't want to be physically fit but financially broke, nor do you desire physical health at the expense of financial stability. You deserve the best of both worlds, and we're here to show you that it's possible.

As living proof that dreams can be realized and goals can be achieved, we raise a toast to you. May you engineer your life by design, carving out a future filled with prosperity and fulfillment.

With unwavering belief in your potential,
Alka Sharma and **Jennifer Nicole Lee**

INTRODUCTION

BY ALKA SHARMA AND JENNIFER NICOLE LEE

Welcome to "The Successful Path to Financial and Physical Fitness: Your Winning Wealth and Health Comprehensive Lifestyle Formula"! We're thrilled to embark on this transformative journey with you, where we'll explore the powerful intersection of financial fitness and physical well-being. As co-authors, Alka Sharma and Jennifer Nicole Lee, we've pooled our expertise together to provide you with a comprehensive blueprint for holistic success.

In today's fast-paced world, it's all too common to find ourselves trapped in the "all or nothing" paradigm. Some of us may excel financially but struggle with our physical health, while others prioritize fitness but neglect our financial futures. But what if we told you that you don't have to choose between the two? That's right – with the right knowledge and mindset, you can achieve both financial prosperity and peak physical fitness.

Throughout this book, you'll discover a wealth of life-changing information that will empower you to unlock your full potential. With over 45 years of combined experience, we've seen firsthand the synergies between financial and physical wellness. By integrating these two aspects of your life, you'll not only build a solid financial foundation but also develop the resilience needed to overcome any obstacles that come your way.

Our goal is simple: to help you create a life where you can truly have it all. Imagine being able to pursue your financial goals with confidence, all while feeling energized, healthy, and strong. This isn't just a pipe dream – it's entirely achievable, and we're here to show you how.

As you embark on this journey, be prepared to challenge old beliefs, embrace new habits, and step outside your comfort zone. Together, we'll explore practical strategies for integrating physical fitness into your daily routine, alongside proven techniques for building wealth and financial security.

Whether you're a seasoned entrepreneur or just starting out on your journey to success, this book is for you. Get ready to discover the secrets to achieving financial success while getting in the best shape of your life. It's time to unleash your full potential – let's dive in! We are so delighted to share our success secrets with you!

Quiz:

Were You Born to be a Wealthy and Healthy Person

1. Do you believe that you deserve to live a life of abundance and prosperity?

2. Are you committed to taking daily actions to improve your financial situation?

3. Do you believe that your health is just as important as your wealth?

4. Are you willing to prioritize self-care and wellness activities in your daily routine?

5. Do you believe that you have the power to create the life you desire?

6. Are you committed to setting and achieving financial goals for yourself?

7. Do you prioritize investing in your physical and mental well-being?

8. Do you believe that you are capable of achieving both financial success and optimal health?

9. Are you willing to let go of limiting beliefs about money and health?

10. Do you take responsibility for your financial decisions and health choices?

11. Do you believe that you are worthy of experiencing both wealth and health?

12. Are you committed to learning and growing in both financial literacy and health knowledge?

13. Do you surround yourself with positive influences that support your goals for wealth and health?

14. Are you open to trying new strategies and techniques to improve your financial and physical well-being?

15. Do you believe that you have the ability to overcome any obstacles that stand in the way of your success?

16. Are you willing to invest time and effort into creating a balanced and fulfilling life?

17. Do you practice gratitude for the wealth and health that you already have in your life?

18. Do you believe that your worth is not determined by your financial status or physical appearance?

19. Are you committed to making choices that align with your values and priorities?

20. Do you believe that you are deserving of a life that is both wealthy and healthy?

After completing the quiz, reflect on your answers to gain insight into your limiting beliefs and commitment level to achieving both your ultimate wealth and health goals.

NOTES:

GAME PLAN

Welcome to a journey that promises not just financial success, but a complete transformation of your well-being. "The Successful Path to Financial and Physical Fitness" isn't just about counting dollars or shedding pounds; it's about embracing abundance in all aspects of your life.

Within these pages, you'll discover the keys to unlocking a mindset that sees opportunities where others see obstacles. You'll explore the core principles of financial literacy, empowering yourself to make informed decisions that pave the way for a secure future. From understanding the basics of budgeting to navigating the complexities of investment, you'll gain the tools needed to take control of your financial destiny.

But true prosperity extends beyond the balance in your bank account. That's why this journey also explores the realm of physical wellness. Through the power of nutrition, exercise, and mindfulness, you'll craft a lifestyle that not only nourishes your body but also nurtures your mind. You'll learn to listen to your body's cues, fueling it with the nutrients it craves and treating it with the care it deserves.

As you progress along this path, you'll encounter challenges—both financial and physical. But armed with the knowledge and resilience gained from these pages, you'll overcome these obstacles with confidence. You'll find yourself embracing empowerment, recognizing that every setback is an opportunity for growth.

This isn't just about reaching a destination—it's about embracing a way of life. Success isn't measured solely by the size of your bank account or the number on the scale; it's about living in alignment with your values and aspirations. It's about finding fulfillment in every aspect of your existence.

So, welcome to your journey to financial and physical fitness—a journey where success isn't just a destination, but a way of life. Together, let's embark on this transformative path towards lasting wealth and health.

Now That You Know You Were Born to be a Wealthy and Healthy VIP Queen Boss Babe, It's Time to Plan Your Work and Work Your Plan!

CONTRACT AND PROMISE TO YOURSELF

Contract and Promise to Myself

"I, [Your Name], hereby solemnly commit to showing up for myself and embarking on a journey of self-discovery and growth in the realms of financial literacy, savings, wealth management, and retirement planning. I recognize the importance of nurturing my financial well-being as a foundation for a prosperous future.

In addition to prioritizing my financial health, I pledge to prioritize my physical and mental well-being. I understand that self-care is not only essential but crucial for achieving holistic balance and fulfillment in life. Therefore, I vow to engage in mindful living, ensuring that I am attentive to both my financial and personal needs.

As I embark on this journey, I embrace the mindset of a business athlete, fully committed to honing my skills and endurance in the pursuit of financial success. I understand that success is not merely about achieving a goal but about the relentless pursuit of improvement and growth. Therefore, I pledge to approach life as if it were a sport, continuously striving to surpass my own limitations and set new standards of excellence.

I acknowledge that challenges will arise along the way, but I am prepared to face them head-on with determination and resilience. I am ready to push myself beyond my comfort zone, knowing that it is through challenges that true growth occurs.

With gratitude for the guidance and support provided by Alka Sharma and Jennifer Nicole Lee, I eagerly anticipate immersing myself in the comprehensive curriculum, courses, and optional coaching offered. I am excited to implement new financial strategies for stability and to embrace a lifestyle of continuous improvement in both my finances and physical fitness.

Signed,

[Your Signature]

Dated,

[Date]"

CHAPTER 1

ALKA SHARMA

BUILDING YOUR FINANCIAL FOUNDATION: FROM BUDGETING TO INVESTING

In this Chapter, I will go over how to get your money to work for you, and why it's important for you to also save money in order to Invest.

On your journey towards financial success, laying down a solid foundation is paramount. Lets dive into the essential steps to establish a robust financial groundwork that sets the stage for wealth generation and long-term stability.

Establishing a strong financial foundation is akin to laying the cornerstone of a sturdy building. Just as a solid foundation provides stability and resilience to a structure, a well-planned financial groundwork empowers individuals and families to weather life's storms and achieve long-term success.

Discipline is the cornerstone of building this foundation. It requires a commitment to thoughtful planning, prudent decision-making, and consistent action. Much like constructing a building, where each brick is carefully laid to ensure structural integrity, every financial decision contributes to the solidity of one's financial structure.

Embarking on this journey towards financial stability and success requires a clear path and a defined destination. Just as a GPS guides us to our desired location, clear financial goals act as beacons, illuminating the path forward. Whether it's saving for a home, funding a child's education, or preparing for retirement, having well-defined goals provides direction and purpose to our financial endeavors.

Moreover, setting clear financial goals is not just about the destination; it's about the journey itself. It's about the sense of empowerment and fulfillment that comes from taking control of one's financial future. Like travelers on a journey, individuals and families navigate through life's twists and turns with confidence, knowing that they are on the right path towards achieving their dreams.

In essence, building a robust financial foundation is about more than just accumulating wealth; it's about creating a life of security, freedom, and fulfillment. It's about laying the groundwork for a future where financial worries are replaced by peace of mind and opportunities for growth and prosperity abound.

The 1st crucial step is to divide money into 3 funds.

1. The Emergency Savings Fund/Account

2. The Investment Fund
3. The Living Fun

The Importance of Budgeting:

Budgeting serves as the cornerstone of financial planning, providing a roadmap for future financial endeavors. By creating a budget, households gain control over their finances, ensuring that money is allocated strategically towards various needs and goals. Much like constructing a sturdy building requires a blueprint, building a financial foundation demands a clear budgeting strategy to guide decision-making and foster discipline.

1. The Emergency Savings Account:

The first step in building a financial fortress is establishing an emergency savings account. This fund acts as a safety net, offering protection against unforeseen circumstances such as job loss or medical emergencies. Determining the appropriate amount to set aside depends on factors such as job security, health status, and individual risk tolerance. By automating contributions to a high-yield savings account, households can gradually build a cushion to weather any financial storm.

The statistics provided by Refresh Financials paint a concerning picture of the financial landscape for many Canadians. It's alarming to learn that more than half of the population is living paycheck to paycheck, leaving them vulnerable to financial emergencies. With a significant portion of respondents lacking savings for emergencies and relying solely on their next paycheck to cover expenses, it's clear that there's a pressing need for greater financial literacy and planning.

Articulating clear financial objectives is the crucial first step towards addressing this issue. By setting specific goals and objectives, individuals can gain a sense of direction and purpose in their financial decisions. Whether it's saving for emergencies, paying off debt, or investing for the future, having clear goals provides a roadmap for making informed financial choices.

Without a clear direction or plan for the future, individuals may find themselves caught in a cycle of financial instability and uncertainty. Without savings or contingency plans in place, unexpected expenses or emergencies can quickly spiral into financial crises, leading to stress, anxiety, and even hardship.

The importance of setting clear financial goals cannot be overstated. They not only provide a sense of direction but also serve as a safeguard against financial pitfalls. By articulating their objectives and taking proactive steps to achieve them, you can take control of their financial futures and work towards a more secure and prosperous life.

The emergency fund is a cornerstone of financial security. To establish a robust emergency fund, several factors need to be considered. First, determine how much money you will need by calculating your living expenses. It's highly recommended to open a high-yield savings account and transfer money into it regularly. This serves as a cushion against unforeseen circumstances, providing a buffer in times of need.

When deciding on the appropriate amount to save for your emergency fund, consider setting aside enough to cover 3-6 months of living expenses. While this range may seem broad, it allows you to tailor your savings goal to your individual circumstances. Factors to consider when determining the size of your emergency fund include the stability of your job, the time it may take to find another job if needed, and your overall health.

By carefully considering these factors and setting aside an appropriate amount of money, you can build a solid emergency fund that provides financial security and peace of mind in times of need.

More food for thought: Consider the stability of your job. If you're a new hire in an industry experiencing layoffs or significant changes, your job security may be uncertain. Assess the likelihood of layoffs or downsizing in your industry to gauge the solidity of your job.

> Evaluate how long it might take to find another job if you were to lose your current one. The longer the job search is expected to be, the greater the risk you face in terms of financial stability. Factors such as the demand for your skills and experience in the job market can influence the duration of your job search.

Assess your health status. If you're at a higher risk of illness or have a medical condition that could lead to extended periods of inability to work, it's important to be financially prepared. On the other hand, if you're at a lower risk of health issues, you may still want to consider setting aside a larger emergency fund to account for potential income loss due to unexpected health challenges. Aim to set aside at least six months' worth of living expenses, and consider increasing it to nine or twelve months if you're at a higher risk or have specific health concerns. By taking these factors into account, you can better prepare yourself financially for any unforeseen circumstances that may arise.

What are your Living Expenses?

Here's how to calculate your living expenses: Multiply the amount by the number of months. For example, if your monthly living expenses total $4,500 and you want to have a savings buffer of 3 months' worth of living expenses, you'll need to set a goal of saving $13,500.

It's important to set specific savings goals to ensure you're adequately prepared for emergencies. One advantageous way to hold your emergency funds is by setting up a high-yield savings account. Automate the process by transferring funds into this account regularly. This ensures that your emergency savings grow steadily while remaining easily accessible when needed.

2. The Investment Fund:

Once the emergency fund is in place, attention turns to the investment fund. This fund represents an opportunity to generate wealth through strategic investments in stocks, real estate, and other assets. By harnessing the power of compounding, families can watch their money grow over time, creating a pathway to financial freedom and security. Discipline and a long-term vision are essential as investments accumulate and produce returns.

Investing in an investment fund allows individuals to grow their wealth over time by harnessing the power of compounding. When money is invested in stock options or shares of companies, it has the potential to appreciate in value and generate additional income through dividends. Similarly, investing in real estate can offer a steady stream of rental income and the potential for property value appreciation.

For many families, financial security and freedom may seem like distant dreams as they struggle to make ends meet. However, by embracing a long-term investment strategy and staying committed to their financial goals, families can overcome financial challenges and build a brighter future for themselves and their loved ones.

3. The Living Fund:

Balancing the present with the future, the living fund covers day-to-day expenses, leisure activities, and discretionary spending. Allocating a portion of income towards savings and investments while living below one's means is crucial for long-term financial success. As investments mature and generate income, households can enjoy greater financial flexibility and autonomy.

Budgeting for Success:

Budgeting is not merely about tracking expenses; it's about aligning financial decisions with long-term goals and values. By regularly reviewing spending habits and making adjustments as needed, families can optimize their finances and stay on track towards achieving their aspirations. Budgeting empowers individuals to make informed choices, prioritize spending, and build wealth systematically.

Conclusion:

Constructing a solid financial foundation requires dedication, discipline, and a clear vision for the future. By implementing sound budgeting practices, establishing emergency savings, and investing strategically, households can pave the way for financial success and security. Each financial decision made today contributes to the strength and resilience of one's financial structure, setting the stage for a prosperous tomorrow.

Step 3: Living fund- This fund money should be allocated for your standard of living, paying bills, ‘fun’ money for leisure and entertainment. Money from earned income allocate 20% towards savings account, 30% allocated towards investing funds, 50% allocated in living fund.

Discipline is required to live below your means to get to a point where your money is compounding giving you an ROI on investments so that you can live comfortably.

Families have to learn money tools required to be financially educated. Making decisions gives them a guide and overview where money is spent.

As your savings accounts amplifies, money can be put towards investment account. This will generate income for families in addition to their job or business. When expenses become problematic you can allocate money from the investment account 50% into the living fund. This is great news every Month. s your investment grows substantially you have more money to work for you. Achieve financial freedom, laying the foundation requires to live below your means so you will have more money to invest for the future.

This is called the 'snowball' effect. Your money grows faster. The questions people should not be asking "what stocks should be deployed" with the money question to ask investing is narrowed down to how you deploy your money which aligns with your goals and give you the ROI.

Implementing right strategies, building right mind set, goals to foresee the future valuing money.

The importance of budgeting, the cornerstone of financial stability. With your goals in sight, this will construct your financial fortress.

This encompasses your income, expenses and saving goals thereby establishing a framework for financial stability by providing a clear overview of your financial landscape. Hereby paying special attention to discretionary spending identify areas where adjustments can be made to strengthen your finances. By implementing these changes allows you to live within your means and it also creates room to save and invest in areas that align with your goals.

The living fund serves as a critical component of your financial strategy. It allows you to maintain your standard of living while also prioritizing savings and investments. This fund should be allocated for essential expenses such as bills and utilities, as well as for discretionary spending on leisure and entertainment activities.

To ensure financial stability and growth, it's recommended to allocate a portion of your earned income towards various financial goals. Typically, 20% is allocated to a savings account for emergencies and short-term goals, while 30% is allocated to an investment fund for long-term wealth building. The remaining 50% is allocated to the living fund to cover day-to-day expenses.

Living below your means is essential to building wealth over time, as it allows your money to compound and generate returns on investments. Families who desire to build wealth must learn effective money management tools and develop financial literacy to make informed decisions about their finances. As your savings grow, you can gradually increase contributions to your investment accounts, generating additional income streams alongside your job or business.

In times of financial strain, such as unexpected expenses or emergencies, you can reallocate funds from your investment accounts to cover living expenses temporarily. This flexibility allows you to maintain financial stability without derailing your long-term financial goals.

The concept of the "snowball effect" illustrates how disciplined saving and investing can lead to exponential growth of your wealth over time. By consistently deploying your money in alignment with your goals and focusing on maximizing returns on investment, you can accelerate your journey towards financial freedom.

Budgeting is the cornerstone of financial stability, providing a clear overview of your income, expenses, and saving goals. By carefully managing your finances and identifying areas where adjustments can be made, you can strengthen your financial position and create room to save and invest while still enjoying a comfortable standard of living.

Constructing a robust financial foundation is akin to building a sturdy structure that can withstand the test of time. It requires a strategic combination of several key elements, each playing a crucial role in shaping your financial future.

First and foremost, setting clear and achievable financial goals is paramount. Whether it's saving for retirement, purchasing a home, or funding your children's education, having defined objectives provides direction and purpose to your financial journey. These goals serve as guiding stars, helping you make informed decisions so that you can stay focused on your long-term vision.

Meticulous budgeting is another essential component of financial success. By carefully tracking your income and expenses, you gain insight into your financial habits and can identify areas where you can cut costs or reallocate resources. A well-crafted budget not only helps you manage your cash flow effectively but also enables you to prioritize savings and investments.

Making informed financial decisions is crucial in developing and elevating your personal finances. This involves conducting thorough research, seeking advice from financial experts, and staying abreast of market trends and economic developments. Whether it's choosing the right investment vehicle, selecting the appropriate insurance coverage, or deciding on the optimal debt repayment strategy, informed decision-making lays the groundwork for financial success.

Continuous learning is a fundamental aspect of maintaining financial health and adaptability. The world of finance is constantly evolving, with new products, technologies, and regulations shaping the way we manage our money. Embracing a mindset of lifelong learning allows you to stay informed about emerging trends, acquire new skills, and adapt to changing circumstances. Whether it's attending workshops, reading financial literature, or participating in online courses, ongoing education empowers you to make informed decisions and seize opportunities for growth.

Ultimately, a solid financial foundation is the cornerstone of reaching new heights of success and security. Every decision you make and every financial habit you cultivate contributes to the strength and resilience of your financial structure. By setting clear goals, practicing meticulous budgeting, making informed choices, and embracing continuous learning, you pave the way for a prosperous and fulfilling financial future.

NOTES:

CHAPTER 2

JENNIFER NICOLE LEE

SCULPTING SUCCESS: THE BLUEPRINT FOR PHYSICAL FITNESS

Welcome to the journey towards sculpting success in your physical fitness journey. I'm Jennifer Nicole Lee, and I've dedicated over two decades of my life to transforming lives globally through wellness and fitness. With a professional background in fitness competitions, I've honed my expertise to guide you on this transformative path.

To embark on this journey, let's lay down some foundational principles. First and foremost, consistency is key. Training 4-6 times per week is optimal, ensuring your body gets the exercise it needs while allowing for essential rest and recovery. Remember, never overdo it—rest is just as crucial as the workout itself. However, the frequency and intensity of your workouts should be tailored to your individual goals, fitness level, and lifestyle. Whether you're aiming to build muscle, lose weight, or improve overall health, finding a sustainable routine that you enjoy is key to long-term success. Additionally, varying your workouts to include different modalities such as strength training, cardio, flexibility, and mobility work can prevent boredom, plateaus, and overuse injuries.

Now, let's explore the triple threat of fitness: weight training, cardio, and recovery. Weight training is essential for building and maintaining muscle mass, which is crucial for boosting metabolism, improving body composition, and enhancing overall strength and functionality. Incorporating a variety of compound and isolation exercises that target different muscle groups ensures balanced development and reduces the risk of imbalances and injuries. Additionally, progressive overload—gradually increasing the resistance or intensity of your workouts over time—is key to stimulating muscle growth and adaptation. Cardiovascular exercise, on the other hand, is vital for improving cardiovascular health, increasing endurance, and burning calories. Whether you prefer high-intensity interval training (HIIT), steady-state cardio, or a combination of both, finding activities that you enjoy and can stick with long-term is essential. Finally, prioritizing rest, recovery, and stretching is often overlooked but equally important for optimal performance and injury prevention. Adequate sleep, proper nutrition, hydration, and stress management are all essential components of the recovery process, allowing your body to repair, regenerate, and adapt to the demands of your workouts.

In the realm of biohacking, utilizing the right supplements can amplify your results in less time. Visit www.JNLBiohack.com for my top recommendations, knowing that proper supplementation can complement your fitness journey. From protein powders to branched-chain amino acids (BCAAs), creatine, and omega-3 fatty acids, these supplements can support muscle growth, improve recovery, and optimize overall health. However, it's essential to consult with a qualified healthcare professional or registered dietitian before adding any new supplements to your regimen, as individual needs and goals may vary. Additionally, focusing on whole foods and a balanced diet rich in lean protein, complex carbohydrates, healthy fats, fruits, vegetables, and hydration should always be the foundation of your nutrition plan.

A coach can be your guiding light on the path to long-term success. In Chapter 3, we'll explore why having a coach is essential, from accountability to personalized guidance. Visit www.JNLCoaching.com to explore how I can support you on your journey. A coach can provide valuable insights, motivation, and accountability, helping you navigate obstacles, overcome plateaus, and stay on track towards your goals. Whether you're a beginner looking to establish a solid foundation or an experienced athlete aiming to break through barriers, a coach can tailor a program to meet your specific needs, preferences, and lifestyle. Additionally, investing in ongoing education, support, and feedback from a coach can accelerate your progress, prevent burnout, and ensure long-term success.

Time management is crucial for balancing physical and financial fitness. Approach your workouts with focus and intensity, ensuring they enhance and not take away productivity. Treat your workout like a vital business meeting—with yourself as the most important attendee. By scheduling your workouts in advance and prioritizing them in your daily routine, you'll ensure consistency and make progress towards your goals. Remember, investing in your health and fitness is an investment in yourself, laying the groundwork for a fulfilling and prosperous life. Additionally, finding efficient and effective ways to integrate physical activity into your daily routine, such as walking or biking instead of driving, taking the stairs instead of the elevator, or incorporating short bursts of activity throughout the day, can help maximize your time and energy.

But beyond individual effort, the power of community cannot be overstated in achieving fitness goals. Studies have shown that those who train in a community or with a workout buddy are more likely to stick with their goals and maintain long-term commitment to their fitness journey. Accountability partners provide support, motivation, and encouragement, helping you stay on track even when motivation wears off. s. Whether it's a friend, family member, or fellow gym-goer, having someone to share your successes, challenges, and progress with can make all the difference.

That's why I've created the JNL VIP Online Coaching Academy at www.JNLVIPSignup.com. It's more than just a coaching program—it's a supportive community with a culture that is non-judgmental and positive. By joining our VIP community, you'll gain access to exclusive workouts, nutrition plans, coaching calls, and a supportive network of like-minded individuals who are committed to achieving their fitness goals. Together, we'll celebrate victories, overcome obstacles, and support each other every step of the way. Join us and experience the power of community in reaching your fullest potential.

As we conclude, remember that sculpting success is important in helping you to build a solid foundation. In the forthcoming chapters, we'll go deeper into nutrition, supplementation, mindset, goal setting, and more. Together, we'll construct a comprehensive framework that withstands the test of time, empowering you to achieve your health and fitness goals and live your best life. Stay tuned as we uncover the strategies, tools, and tactics for creating lasting change and sustainable results.

Bonus tip: Use a calendar to schedule your workouts, treating them as non-negotiable appointments with yourself. By committing to your fitness journey, you're investing in your most valuable asset—you. With dedication, determination, and the right guidance, you can sculpt the body and life of your dreams. Let's embark on this journey together, one workout at a time.

NOTES:

CHAPTER 3

ALKA SHARMA

GROWING YOUR WEALTH: STRATEGIES FOR FINANCIAL HEALTH & THE BASICS OF REAL ESTATE INVESTING

If you aspire to achieve financial freedom and earn passive income, understanding the role of money as a tool is essential.

Money serves three primary purposes:

1. Saving
2. Spending
3. Investing.

Achieving a balance between these three aspects is crucial to ensure that your financial resources are utilized effectively and not squandered.

Saving money is important, but it should be done with purpose. Simply hoarding money without a clear reason or goal in mind can be counterproductive. Instead, savings should be directed towards specific objectives, such as building an emergency fund, saving for a down payment on a home, or funding retirement. By assigning a purpose to your savings, you give your money direction and ensure that it is working towards your long-term financial goals.

Spending money wisely is also key to financial success. While it's important to enjoy the fruits of your labor and indulge in occasional luxuries, overspending can quickly derail your financial plans. Practicing mindful spending involves distinguishing between needs and wants, prioritizing essential expenses, and avoiding unnecessary purchases. By exercising restraint and making thoughtful spending decisions, you can maximize the value of your money and avoid falling into debt traps.

Investing is perhaps the most powerful wealth-building tool available. By putting your money to work in various investment vehicles, such as stocks, bonds, real estate, or business ventures, you have the potential to generate passive income and grow your wealth over time. However, investing requires careful consideration and risk management. It's essential to conduct thorough research, diversify your investments, and seek professional advice when necessary to make informed decisions and mitigate risks.

Achieving financial freedom and earning passive income requires a balanced approach to managing your money. By saving with purpose, spending wisely, and investing prudently, you can leverage your financial resources to create a more secure and prosperous future.

Outlined below are tips for wealth creation:

Job: Have you ever considered quitting your job to live off your investments and pursue your passions, achieving financial freedom and happiness? While many dream of this lifestyle, few achieve it. Why? Because they lack a solid foundation of income and savings and fail to develop a plan to grow their wealth and live off their investments. Building a solid foundation of wealth is a step-by-step process—it doesn't happen overnight but rather over time. Achieving financial freedom is a long-term goal that requires patience and persistence.

The challenging aspect of building wealth is knowing what you want in the future. Take the time to envision your life a few years, 10 years, and 20 years from now, working towards achieving goals that bring you closer to your vision.

Save: Allocate a portion of your income towards savings. Imagine living a life where you can do anything you want, travel the world, and spend time with loved ones. Achieving financial independence and growing wealth to live off investments is possible. The key lies in saving a significant portion of your income each month and investing it wisely to generate passive income.

Passive income allows you to earn money while you sleep, and it can be derived from various sources such as dividend stocks, interest, rent, and royalties. By building a portfolio of passive income streams, you pave the way to retire early while continuing to save and invest. Consider investing in dividend stocks, which are stable, well-established, and profitable companies. Wealth creation is challenging but possible with patience, discipline, and knowledge. Cut down on unnecessary spending and focus on boosting earnings through strategic investments.

These tips represent sound investing principles that must be diligently and consistently applied to achieve financial freedom. It requires patience, persistence, and discipline over time. Work hard, continuously learn new skills, and take control of your destiny.

Don't wait for tomorrow to start your financial journey—make every day count towards building the future you envision.

Ask yourself this question, would you prefer to appear wealthy or actually possess wealth? The answer is likely the latter—to truly be rich. It's essential that your lifestyle aligns with the values you express. While your current ideal life may involve shopping at luxury stores like Gucci, owning Rolex watches, and carrying Louis Vuitton accessories, there's a crucial caveat to consider.

If you indulge in a designer lifestyle without simultaneously building an investment portfolio, you might only appear rich in the short term while inadvertently enriching others. It's important to recognize that true wealth isn't just about material possessions or flashy displays of affluence. Instead, it's about having financial security and freedom, which can only be achieved through prudent financial planning and strategic investing.

While there's nothing inherently wrong with enjoying luxury goods, it's vital to prioritize long-term financial stability over fleeting displays of wealth. By investing in assets that generate passive income and appreciating value over time, you can build genuine wealth that provides security and opportunities for a prosperous future.

While it's tempting to pursue a lavish lifestyle, true richness comes from aligning your actions with your financial goals and investing in your future rather than simply indulging in conspicuous consumption.

What distinguishes millionaires and wealthy individuals from the financially insecure is their practice of paying themselves first and prioritizing the acquisition of assets that generate income. It's important to understand that wealth begins with a mindset—a wealthy mindset precedes wealth in one's bank account. The secret to financial success lies in the realization that assets can fund a luxurious lifestyle, and the wealthy understand this game well.

To illustrate this further, consider opening three separate bank accounts:

- **Spending Account - 75%:** This account is designated for day-to-day expenses and discretionary spending.

- **Investing Account - 15%:** Allocate a portion of your income to investments that have the potential to grow over time and generate passive income.

- **Saving Account - 10%:** Set aside a portion of your earnings for short-term goals and emergency funds.

By segregating your funds into these distinct accounts, you can prevent accidental spending of your savings and ensure that your financial priorities are clear. It's advisable to automate your deposits into these accounts to ensure consistent contributions.

The key principle behind this strategy is to pay yourself first—prioritize allocating money towards investments, savings, and then spending. Now that we've established the framework, it's time to accelerate your path to wealth. You may wonder how to do this. Consider adopting an aggressive investment approach, allocating a larger percentage of your income (such as 30-70%) towards investments. Remember, there's no limit to how much you can earn through strategic investments.

By taking control of your finances, growing your income, and shifting your mindset, you can increase your earning potential and move closer to achieving financial freedom. It's not just about accumulating wealth; it's about leveraging your resources to create a life of abundance and fulfillment.

Building wealth is a journey that requires time, effort, and discipline. The first step is to ensure that you're earning enough to cover your basic needs while leaving room for savings. By managing your spending wisely, you can maximize your savings and pave the way towards investing in various assets for the long term.

Here are 7 Key Principles to Building Wealth:

1. Earning Money: The foundation of wealth-building begins with earning income. While this may seem obvious, even small amounts saved and compounded over time can grow into significant sums. Consider both earned income from your work and passive income from investments.

2. Setting Goals: Develop a clear plan for your wealth. Identify what you want to achieve—whether it's funding your child's education, planning for retirement (perhaps even early retirement), or contributing to charitable causes. Having a specific vision allows you to create a realistic budget focused on long-term objectives.

4. Saving Money: Simply earning money isn't enough to build wealth if you spend it all. Prioritize saving for near-term obligations such as bills, mortgage payments, and emergencies. Consider strategies

like tracking your spending, distinguishing between needs and wants, and setting monthly savings goals.

5. Investing: Once you've accumulated savings, the next step is to invest wisely. Diversify your investments across stocks, bonds, and other assets to maximize returns over time.

6. Protecting Your Assets: It's crucial to safeguard the wealth you've worked hard to accumulate. Consider insurance policies that would replace your income in the event of injury or loss.

7. Minimizing Tax Impact: Taxes can significantly impact your wealth-building efforts. Work with a qualified tax accountant to develop strategies for minimizing tax liabilities based on your financial situation.

8. Managing Debt and Building Credit: As you build wealth, you may take on debt to fund investments or make purchases. While using credit cards for rewards can be advantageous, it's essential to manage debt carefully. Pay off high-interest debts promptly to avoid excessive interest charges and maintain a healthy credit score.

By following these principles and remaining disciplined in your financial approach, you can navigate the path to wealth with confidence and achieve your long-term financial goals. Remember, wealth-building is not just about accumulating money—it's about securing your financial future and living a life of abundance and security.

NOTES:

CHAPTER 4

JENNIFER NICOLE LEE

FUELING YOUR BODY: NUTRITION ESSENTIALS FOR OPTIMAL FITNESS

Welcome to Chapter 4 of "The Successful Path to Financial and Physical Fitness: Your Winning Wealth and Health Comprehensive Lifestyle Formula." In this chapter, we consider the crucial aspect of nutrition and its profound impact on achieving optimal physical fitness. I'm thrilled to guide you through the essential principles and practices of fueling your body for success. Plus, I will cover my favorite ways to biohack your biology with the best scientifically proven supplements on the market! Let's eat our way to optimal health! Remember, abs are made in the kitchen!

In order to be truly wealthy, you must eat healthy! Both Alka and I know the importance of proper nutrition! But being a busy business owner and entrepreneur, we know that we can sometimes skip meals just to save time. But, this is a self-defeating habit. And it must end today! You need a solid foundation to win in life, and just like a home, it too needs a solid foundation to stand the test of time. Nutrition serves as the foundation upon which your fitness goals are built. Just as a car requires quality fuel to perform optimally, your body requires essential nutrients to function at its best. Imagine your body as a finely tuned machine, with each nutrient playing a crucial role in its operation.

Proper nutrition not only fuels your workouts but also aids in recovery, promotes muscle growth, and supports overall health and well-being. Let's explore in more detail how nutrition impacts various aspects of physical fitness:

- **Fueling Workouts:** Carbohydrates are the primary fuel source for your muscles during exercise. Consuming adequate carbohydrates before a workout provides your body with the energy it needs to perform optimally. Additionally, protein consumption before exercise can help prevent muscle breakdown and improve muscle repair during and after your workout.

- **Aiding in Recovery:** After intense exercise, your muscles need to repair and rebuild. Consuming a combination of carbohydrates and protein post-workout helps replenish glycogen stores and stimulates muscle protein synthesis, facilitating faster recovery and reducing muscle soreness.

- **Promoting Muscle Growth:** Protein is essential for muscle repair and growth. When you engage in strength training or resistance exercises, you create micro-tears in your muscle fibers. Consuming adequate protein post-workout provides your muscles with the building blocks they need to repair and grow stronger.

- **Supporting Overall Health and Well-being:** Proper nutrition is not just about fueling your workouts; it's about nourishing your body to support optimal function and longevity. A balanced diet rich in fruits, vegetables, whole grains, lean proteins, and healthy fats provides essential vitamins, minerals, and antioxidants that support immune function, heart health, brain function, and more.

By prioritizing nutrition and fueling your body with the right foods at the right times, you can maximize your performance, accelerate your progress towards your fitness goals, and enhance your overall quality of life. Remember, nutrition is not a one-size-fits-all approach. Experiment with different foods and meal timings to find what works best for your body and lifestyle. With consistency and mindful eating habits, you can unlock your full potential and achieve lasting success in your fitness journey.

This is why I love teaching workouts and how to eat healthy, seeing so many crack their wealth and health codes just through eating like an athlete, to become better business athletes!

Macronutrients: The Building Blocks of Nutrition

Just like a builder builds a home, and a business owner builds their business, we too must build our bodies! One brick, business deal and meal at a time!

Protein:

Protein is often hailed as the king of macronutrients for fitness enthusiasts, and for good reason. It's vital for repairing and building muscle tissue, making it indispensable for anyone seeking to improve their fitness levels. When you engage in physical activity, especially strength training or resistance exercises, you create microscopic tears in your muscle fibers. Protein consumption provides the necessary amino acids your body needs to repair these tears, leading to muscle growth and strength gains over time.

Incorporate lean sources of protein into your meals to support muscle repair and growth. Some excellent sources of lean protein include:

- Chicken: Skinless chicken breast is a lean protein option that is low in fat and high in quality protein.
- Fish: Fatty fish like salmon, trout, and mackerel not only provide protein but also healthy omega-3 fatty

acids, which have anti-inflammatory properties and support heart health.

- Tofu: Tofu is a versatile plant-based protein option that is rich in protein and low in saturated fat.

- Beans and Lentils: Legumes like beans and lentils are affordable, nutrient-dense sources of protein, fiber, and various vitamins and minerals.

Including a source of protein in each meal and snack can help keep you feeling satisfied, promote muscle recovery, and support your fitness goals.

Carbohydrates:

Carbohydrates are your body's primary source of energy, especially during exercise. They provide the fuel your muscles need to perform optimally during workouts, whether you're lifting weights, running, or participating in any other physical activity. While low-carb diets have gained popularity in recent years, carbohydrates are essential for maintaining energy levels, supporting brain function, and preserving muscle glycogen stores.

Opt for complex carbohydrates like whole grains, fruits, vegetables, and legumes, which provide sustained energy levels and essential nutrients. These carbohydrates are digested more slowly than simple carbohydrates like sugar and refined grains, resulting in more stable blood sugar levels and prolonged energy release.

Some excellent sources of complex carbohydrates include:

- Whole Grains: Choose whole grain options like brown rice, quinoa, oats, and whole wheat bread and pasta for fiber, vitamins, and minerals.

- Fruits: Incorporate a variety of fruits into your diet, such as berries, bananas, apples, and oranges, which provide natural sugars, fiber, and antioxidants.

- Vegetables: Fill your plate with colorful vegetables like spinach, broccoli, bell peppers, carrots, and sweet potatoes, which are rich in vitamins, minerals, and phytonutrients.

- Legumes: Beans, lentils, and chickpeas are excellent sources of both protein and carbohydrates, making them a nutritious addition to salads, soups, and stews.

By including complex carbohydrates in your meals and snacks, you can provide your body with the sustained energy it needs to power through workouts and support your overall health and well-being.

Fats:

Contrary to popular belief, fats are not the enemy when it comes to nutrition. Healthy fats play a crucial role in hormone production, joint health, brain function, and overall well-being. Including sources of unsaturated fats in your diet can help support heart health, reduce inflammation, and promote satiety.

Some sources of healthy fats include:

- Avocados: Avocados are rich in monounsaturated fats, fiber, and various vitamins and minerals. Add sliced avocado to salads, sandwiches, or smoothies for a creamy texture and added nutrients.

- Nuts and Seeds: Almonds, walnuts, chia seeds, flaxseeds, and hemp seeds are all excellent sources of healthy fats, protein, and fiber. Sprinkle them on top of yogurt, oatmeal, or salads for a crunchy texture and nutty flavor.

- Olive Oil: Extra virgin olive oil is a staple of the Mediterranean diet and is prized for its high content of monounsaturated fats and antioxidants. Use olive oil for cooking, salad dressings, or drizzling over roasted vegetables for added flavor and nutrition.

While healthy fats are beneficial for overall health, it's essential to moderate your intake of saturated and trans fats, which can contribute to heart disease and other health issues. Limit your consumption of foods high in saturated and trans fats, such as fried foods, processed snacks, and fatty cuts of meat.

By incorporating a balance of protein, carbohydrates, and healthy fats into your diet, you can fuel your body for optimal performance, support muscle growth and recovery, and enhance your overall health and well-being. Remember to prioritize whole, nutrient-dense foods and listen to your body's hunger and fullness cues to guide your eating habits. With a mindful approach to nutrition, you can achieve your fitness goals and thrive both inside and outside the gym.

Micronutrients: The Nutritional Powerhouses

Vitamins:

Vitamins are essential organic compounds that your body needs in small amounts to function properly. They play a crucial role in various bodily functions, including energy metabolism, immune support, and bone health. While vitamins are not a direct source of energy like macronutrients, they act as cofactors for enzymatic reactions that facilitate energy production and metabolism.

Here are some key vitamins and their roles in the body:

- Vitamin A: Supports vision, immune function, and skin health. Sources include carrots, sweet potatoes, spinach, and kale.

- Vitamin C: Acts as an antioxidant, supports immune function, and aids in collagen production. Found in citrus fruits, strawberries, bell peppers, and broccoli.

- Vitamin D: Facilitates calcium absorption, supports bone health, and regulates immune function. Sunlight exposure and fortified foods like dairy products and fortified cereals are sources of vitamin D.

- Vitamin E: Functions as an antioxidant, protecting cells from damage, and supports immune function. Food sources include nuts, seeds, vegetable oils, and leafy greens.

- Vitamin K: Essential for blood clotting and bone health. Leafy greens, broccoli, Brussels sprouts, and fermented foods like sauerkraut are sources of vitamin K.

To ensure you're meeting your vitamin requirements, consume a diverse array of fruits, vegetables, and whole foods. Aim to include a variety of colorful fruits and vegetables in your diet to maximize your intake of vitamins and other beneficial phytonutrients.

Minerals:

Minerals are inorganic compounds that play essential roles in various physiological processes in the body. They are critical for maintaining strong bones, supporting muscle function, regulating fluid balance, and facilitating oxygen transport. While your body requires larger amounts of certain minerals like calcium and magnesium, others, such as iron and zinc, are needed in smaller quantities but are equally important for overall health.

Here are some key minerals and their roles in the body:

- Calcium: Vital for bone health, muscle function, nerve transmission, and blood clotting. Dairy products, leafy greens, fortified foods, and nuts are sources of calcium.

- Magnesium: Supports muscle and nerve function, regulates blood sugar levels, and contributes to bone health. Sources include leafy greens, nuts, seeds, whole grains, and legumes.

- Iron: Necessary for oxygen transport in the blood and energy metabolism. Red meat, poultry, fish, lentils, beans, and fortified cereals are sources of iron.

- Zinc: Supports immune function, wound healing, and DNA synthesis. Food sources include meat, shellfish, legumes, nuts, seeds, and dairy products.

Incorporating mineral-rich foods like leafy greens, nuts, seeds, dairy products, and legumes into your diet can help ensure you're meeting your mineral requirements. Additionally, pairing iron-rich foods with sources of vitamin C can enhance iron absorption, promoting optimal nutrient utilization in the body.

By prioritizing a varied and nutrient-dense diet that includes a wide range of fruits, vegetables, whole grains, lean proteins, and healthy fats, you can support your body's micronutrient needs and promote overall health and well-being. Remember, micronutrients work synergistically with macronutrients to optimize physiological function, so aim for balance and diversity in your dietary choices.

Hydration: The Key to Peak Performance

Staying hydrated is not only fundamental for optimal physical performance but also essential for overall well-being. Water is often referred to as the elixir of life because of its critical role in regulating various bodily functions. Proper hydration is vital for maintaining body temperature, supporting digestion, lubricating joints, cushioning organs, and transporting nutrients and oxygen throughout the body.

Here are some key reasons why hydration is crucial for peak performance and overall health:

Regulating Body Temperature:

During exercise, your body produces heat as a byproduct of muscle contraction. Sweating is the body's natural mechanism for dissipating heat and regulating body temperature. However, excessive sweating can lead to dehydration if fluids and electrolytes are not replenished adequately. Staying hydrated helps maintain fluid balance, allowing your body to effectively regulate temperature and prevent overheating during physical activity.

Supporting Digestion:

Water is essential for proper digestion and nutrient absorption. It helps break down food particles, facilitates the transport of nutrients across the intestinal wall, and aids in the elimination of waste products. Adequate hydration promotes regular bowel movements and prevents constipation, ensuring optimal digestive function and nutrient utilization.

Transporting Nutrients:

Water serves as the primary medium for transporting nutrients, hormones, and oxygen throughout the body. It helps dissolve and carry nutrients from the digestive system to cells, where they are used for energy production, muscle repair, and various physiological processes. Proper hydration ensures efficient nutrient delivery to cells, supporting energy metabolism and overall health.

Maintaining Fluid Balance:

Fluid balance is essential for maintaining proper blood volume, blood pressure, and electrolyte balance in the body. Dehydration can disrupt fluid balance, leading to decreased blood volume, impaired circulation, and electrolyte imbalances. By staying hydrated, you can support optimal blood flow, nutrient delivery, and cellular function, enhancing physical performance and recovery.

How Much Water Should You Drink?

The general recommendation is to aim for at least eight glasses of water per day, but individual fluid needs vary based on factors such as body size, activity level, climate, and overall health status. Athletes and individuals engaging in vigorous exercise may need to consume more water to replace fluids lost through sweat and exertion. Additionally, environmental factors such as heat and humidity can increase fluid requirements, necessitating adjustments in hydration strategies.

To determine your fluid needs, consider the following guidelines:

- Monitor Urine Color: Aim for pale yellow urine, which indicates adequate hydration. Darker urine may signal dehydration and the need to increase fluid intake.

- Listen to Your Body: Pay attention to thirst cues and drink water regularly throughout the day, especially during and after exercise.

- Weigh Yourself: Monitor changes in body weight before and after exercise to estimate fluid losses. Aim to replace lost fluids by consuming 16-24 ounces of water for every pound lost during exercise.

Incorporating Hydration Strategies:

To stay adequately hydrated, consider incorporating the following hydration strategies into your daily routine:

- Carry a Water Bottle: Keep a reusable water bottle with you throughout the day to encourage regular hydration and make it convenient to drink water whenever you're thirsty.

- Sip Water Before, During, and After Exercise: Hydrate before, during, and after exercise to replace fluids lost through sweat and maintain optimal performance and recovery.

- Flavor Water with Fruit: Add natural flavor to water by infusing it with fresh fruit slices, such as lemon, lime, cucumber, or berries, to enhance taste and encourage consumption.

- Monitor Electrolyte Intake: In addition to water, consider consuming electrolyte-rich beverages or snacks during prolonged exercise or in hot environments to replace lost sodium, potassium, and other electrolytes.

By prioritizing hydration and making conscious efforts to drink enough water throughout the day, you can support optimal physical performance, enhance recovery, and promote overall health and well-being. Remember, hydration is a continuous process, so listen to your body's thirst signals and adjust your fluid intake accordingly to stay adequately hydrated and energized for whatever challenges lie ahead.

Meal Timing and Portion Control

Pre-Workout Nutrition:

Fueling your body with the right nutrients before exercise is essential for optimizing performance and supporting muscle function. Aim to consume a balanced meal or snack containing carbohydrates and protein about 1-2 hours before your workout. This timing allows for adequate digestion and absorption of nutrients, providing sustained energy throughout your exercise session.

Some pre-workout snack options include:

- Banana with almond butter: Bananas are rich in carbohydrates for quick energy, while almond butter provides protein and healthy fats to support sustained energy and muscle repair.

- Greek yogurt with berries: Greek yogurt is high in protein and also contains carbohydrates, making it an excellent pre-workout option. Add some berries for additional flavor and antioxidants.

If you have less time before your workout or prefer something lighter, opt for a smaller snack such as a piece of fruit, a handful of nuts, or a protein shake.

Post-Workout Nutrition:

After exercise, your body needs to replenish glycogen stores and support muscle recovery to facilitate optimal recovery and adaptation to training. Consuming a combination of carbohydrates and protein within 30-60 minutes post-workout is ideal for maximizing these benefits.

Consider the following post-workout meal options:

- Protein shake with fruit: Blend whey protein powder with water or milk and add some fruit for carbohydrates and flavor. This convenient option provides a quick and easily digestible source of protein and carbohydrates to kickstart recovery.

- Turkey sandwich on whole grain bread: Turkey is a lean source of protein, while whole grain bread provides carbohydrates and fiber. Add some vegetables like lettuce, tomato, and avocado for added nutrients and flavor.

- Chicken and vegetable stir-fry: Cook up some chicken breast with mixed vegetables and serve over brown rice or quinoa for a balanced post-workout meal. This option provides a combination of protein, carbohydrates, and micronutrients to support recovery and refuel your body.

Portion Control:

Maintaining portion control is key to managing caloric intake, preventing overeating, and maintaining a healthy weight. While nutrient timing and food choices are important, portion sizes also play a significant role in achieving your fitness goals.

Here are some tips for practicing portion control:

- Use visual cues: Familiarize yourself with recommended serving sizes for different food groups and use visual cues to estimate portion sizes. For example, a serving of meat is about the size of a deck of cards, while a serving of grains is about the size of a tennis ball.

- Plate balance: Aim to fill half your plate with vegetables, a quarter with protein, and a quarter with carbohydrates. This balanced approach ensures you're getting a variety of nutrients and helps prevent overeating.
- Listen to your body: Pay attention to your body's hunger and fullness signals and eat until you're satisfied, not overly full. Eating slowly and mindfully can help you tune into these cues and prevent overeating.

By practicing mindful eating habits, paying attention to portion sizes, and timing your meals and snacks strategically around your workouts, you can optimize nutrient intake, support performance and recovery, and achieve your fitness goals more effectively. Remember, consistency is key, so aim to make these habits a regular part of your routine for long-term success.

Creating a Sustainable Nutrition Plan

Achieving optimal fitness requires more than just short-term dietary changes; it requires a sustainable approach to nutrition that aligns with your goals, preferences, and lifestyle. A sustainable nutrition plan is one that you can maintain over the long term, allowing you to achieve and maintain your desired level of fitness while enjoying a balanced and varied diet.

Here are some key principles for creating a sustainable nutrition plan:

Experimentation and Flexibility:

Everyone's nutritional needs and preferences are unique, so it's essential to experiment with different meal plans, recipes, and eating patterns to find what works best for you. This might involve trying different macronutrient ratios, exploring new foods and cuisines, or experimenting with intermittent fasting or other eating patterns. Be open to trying new things and be willing to adjust your approach based on how your body responds.

Focus on Whole, Nutrient-Dense Foods:

Aim to nourish your body with whole, nutrient-dense foods that provide a wide range of vitamins, minerals, antioxidants, and other beneficial compounds. These foods include fruits, vegetables, whole grains, lean proteins, healthy fats, and legumes. By prioritizing these nutrient-rich foods, you can ensure that your body receives the essential nutrients it needs to function optimally and support your fitness goals.

Plan Ahead and Meal Prep:

One of the keys to maintaining a healthy diet is planning ahead and preparing meals and snacks in advance. Set aside time each week to plan your meals, create a grocery list, and prepare ingredients or full meals ahead of time. This can help you avoid relying on convenience foods or unhealthy options when you're busy or stressed, making it easier to stick to your nutrition plan.

Practice Mindful Eating:

Mindful eating involves paying attention to the food you're eating, savoring each bite, and listening to your body's hunger and fullness cues. By eating slowly, chewing your food thoroughly, and focusing on the sensory experience of eating, you can improve digestion, prevent overeating, and develop a healthier relationship with food. Try to minimize distractions while eating, such as watching TV or scrolling on your phone, and tune into your body's signals to guide your eating habits.

Allow for Flexibility and Enjoyment:

While it's essential to prioritize nutrient-dense foods, it's also important to allow for flexibility and enjoyment in your diet. This might mean incorporating occasional treats or indulgences, dining out with friends and family, or enjoying your favorite foods in moderation. Depriving yourself of foods you love can lead to feelings of restriction and ultimately derail your nutrition plan. By allowing yourself to enjoy a balanced and varied diet that includes foods you love, you can maintain a sustainable approach to nutrition over the long term.

Seek Support and Accountability:

Finally, don't hesitate to seek support and accountability from friends, family, or a qualified nutrition professional. Having a support system can help you stay motivated, overcome challenges, and stay on track with your nutrition goals. Consider joining a fitness community, participating in group challenges, or working with a registered dietitian or nutrition coach who can provide personalized guidance and support.

By incorporating these principles into your nutrition plan, you can create a sustainable approach to eating that supports your fitness goals, enhances your overall health and well-being, and allows you to enjoy a balanced and fulfilling diet for years to come. Remember, achieving optimal fitness is not just about what you eat but also how you nourish your body and prioritize your overall wellness.

In conclusion nutrition is a cornerstone of physical fitness, providing the fuel your body needs to thrive and achieve your fitness goals. By prioritizing a balanced diet rich in macronutrients, micronutrients, and hydration, you can optimize your performance, enhance recovery, and support long-term health and well-being. Remember, success begins with the choices you make each day, so fuel your body wisely and reap the rewards of a healthier, happier you.

NOTES:

CHAPTER 5

ALKA SHARMA

INVESTING IN YOUR FUTURE: CREATING SUSTAINABLE FINANCIAL HABITS AND ESSENTIAL TIPS FOR SUCCESSFUL REAL ESTATE INVESTING

Financial planning is the blueprint for a secure and prosperous future. It involves much more than just setting aside a portion of your income for savings—it's a comprehensive strategy that encompasses setting realistic goals, creating budgets, managing debt effectively, and making informed investment decisions.

Setting Realistic Goals: One of the first steps in financial planning is defining your long-term objectives. Whether it's buying a home, funding your children's education, or retiring comfortably, establishing clear and achievable goals provides direction and purpose to your financial journey.

Creating a Budget: A budget acts as a roadmap for your finances, guiding your spending and saving habits. By carefully allocating funds to different categories such as housing, utilities, groceries, and entertainment, you can ensure that your financial resources are utilized efficiently and effectively.

Managing Debt: Debt can be a significant obstacle to financial security if not managed properly. As part of your financial plan, it's essential to develop strategies for paying down existing debt and avoiding unnecessary borrowing. By prioritizing high-interest debt and making consistent payments, you can reduce your debt burden over time and free up resources for other financial goals.

Investing Wisely: Investing is a crucial component of long-term wealth accumulation. A well-thought-out investment strategy tailored to your risk tolerance, time horizon, and financial goals can help grow your wealth over time. Whether it's stocks, bonds, real estate, or other assets, diversifying your investments can mitigate risk and maximize returns.

Without a solid financial plan in place, it's easy to lose sight of your financial priorities and miss out on opportunities for growth. By taking the time to develop and implement a comprehensive financial plan, you can take control of your finances, build a secure future, and achieve your financial aspirations.

Investing is a fundamental strategy for building wealth and securing your financial future. At its core, investing involves putting your money to work in assets that have the potential to grow over time, thereby generating returns and increasing your wealth.

One of the key benefits of investing is the power of compounding. When you invest your money, you not only earn returns on your initial investment but also on any returns that are reinvested. Over time, this compounding effect can significantly increase the value of your investment portfolio, allowing your money to grow exponentially.

Moreover, investing provides a hedge against inflation, which erodes the purchasing power of your savings over time. By allocating your funds to assets that have the potential to outpace inflation, such as stocks, real estate, or commodities, you can preserve and even enhance the value of your wealth in the long run.

Additionally, investing can help you achieve financial goals that may seem out of reach through savings alone. Whether it's funding your children's education, buying a home, or retiring comfortably, investing can provide the means to realize these objectives and enjoy a more financially secure future.

However, investing involves risks, and it's essential to approach it with careful consideration and planning. Diversifying your investment portfolio, conducting thorough research, and seeking professional advice can help mitigate risks and maximize returns.

Investing is a vital component of any comprehensive financial plan. By harnessing the power of compounding and strategically allocating your funds to assets with growth potential, you can build wealth, achieve your financial goals, and secure a more comfortable and confident future.

Achieving financial freedom isn't a matter of luck or privilege; it's about breaking free from ingrained money habits that have held you back. Rather than viewing money as a constraint, it should be seen as a tool that can amplify your financial situation.

Developing a wealth-building mindset is the first step toward financial freedom. This involves shifting perspectives and challenging limiting beliefs that may have been ingrained since childhood. Phrases like "I'll never be wealthy" or "I don't deserve money" can create mental barriers that hinder progress. Breaking free from these limiting beliefs is essential to achieving financial success.

Let's bid farewell to financial struggles! While payday often brings excitement and the temptation to indulge in treats, it's crucial to resist the urge to splurge recklessly. Many individuals fall into the trap of living paycheck to paycheck, following the crowd's spending habits without considering the long-term consequences.

In this section, I'll outline five common mistakes to avoid when you receive your paycheck. It's time to adopt a different mindset and make smarter spending decisions that align with your financial goals. By thinking differently about how you manage your money, you can pave the way toward financial security and abundance.

Receiving a paycheck can indeed be exhilarating—it's the tangible reward for your hard work and dedication. However, it's common for individuals to fall into the trap of immediately allocating their earnings toward essential expenses like rent and bills, with little consideration for their own financial well-being.

One prevalent but detrimental money habit is paying oneself last. After covering necessary expenses and saving a portion of their income, many people find themselves with little to no discretionary funds left for personal enjoyment or investment. Instead of celebrating their financial achievements or using their earnings to pursue their goals, they end up feeling restricted and limited in their options.

To break free from this cycle, it's essential to prioritize paying yourself first. This means setting aside a portion of your paycheck for personal use or investment before allocating funds to other expenses. By adopting this approach, you empower yourself to take control of your financial future and make intentional decisions about how you use your money.

Whether it's treating yourself to a well-deserved reward, investing in your education or personal growth, or contributing to your long-term financial goals, paying yourself first allows you to align your spending with your values and aspirations. It's a crucial step toward building a healthy relationship with money and achieving greater financial security and abundance.

NOT HAVING A STOCKPILE –

Essentially, you want to save enough money to create a cushion, a buffer of at least 3-6 months' worth of expenses. This is crucial because it provides peace of mind knowing that you have funds set aside and readily available when needed.

To build this buffer, start by putting away 10% of your income into a savings account. The additional funds can then be allocated towards investments or other financial goals.

Rich people have different habits when it comes to managing their finances. They prioritize paying themselves first by depositing a portion of their income, typically around 10%, into their savings account. This approach ensures that money is not easily spent on unnecessary expenses and helps to build a solid financial foundation for the future.

GETTING COMFORTABLE WITH BAD DEBT —

Debt seems to be the norm for many people, with credit cards often being used to finance purchases that exceed their current means. This reliance on debt can quickly spiral out of control, leading to financial stress and uncertainty.

To break free from this cycle, it's essential to adopt a mindset of financial discipline and responsibility. Rather than viewing debt as a convenient way to afford luxuries in the present, consider the long-term implications of carrying debt.

One helpful strategy is to establish clear criteria for when it's appropriate to use debt. For example, only consider taking on debt for essential purchases or investments that have the potential to generate long-term returns. Remember the golden rule: if you can't afford to buy 5 of any item, you can't afford one.

Additionally, prioritize paying down existing debt to reduce interest costs and free up more of your income for savings and investments. By actively managing your debt and avoiding unnecessary borrowing, you can take control of your financial future and build a solid foundation for long-term prosperity.

CLIFF SPENDER PHENOMENON —

The majority of people find themselves living paycheck to paycheck, often succumbing to impulsive spending habits that leave them financially stranded until the next payday.

It's crucial to recognize and address this pattern to regain control of your finances and work towards a more stable financial future.

One effective strategy is to create a detailed budget using tools like an Excel spreadsheet. Start by listing your income at the top and then break down all your expenses below. This allows you to see exactly where your money is going and identify areas where you can make adjustments to avoid overspending.

By keeping a constant eye on your financial transactions, you empower yourself to make better decisions about how to allocate your resources. This not only helps you avoid unnecessary expenses but also allows you to prioritize saving and investing for the future.

True financial freedom stems from building wealth rather than indulging in impulsive spending on wants rather than needs. It's important to recognize the allure of retail therapy and the billions of dollars spent by companies to tempt us into spending money.

Instead of splurging on temporary indulgences, consider investing in yourself for long-term growth and fulfillment. Celebrate your financial milestones with meaningful experiences that enrich your life and provide lasting satisfaction, whether through saving, investing, or simply appreciating the security of your income.

NOT KNOWING YOUR INCOME AND EXPENSES —

Understanding your starting point is essential for navigating your financial journey. Without a clear picture of your income and expenses, it's challenging to make informed decisions about your finances. One common trap many fall into is lifestyle inflation, where spending increases along with income. As you earn more, you may find yourself spending more, often exceeding your means in a cycle that can lead to financial strain.

To take control of your finances, it's crucial to map out where your money is being spent. Using a budget tracker can be an excellent tool for this purpose, helping you visualize your income, expenses, bills, mortgage payments, and debt repayments. This process requires discipline and consistent management of your finances for at least three months to accurately assess your financial situation.

Individuals who have a clear understanding of their financial status, including their assets and liabilities, are better equipped to set achievable goals and develop a plan for their financial future. By having a clear direction and a well-defined plan, you can avoid falling into the trap of merely dreaming about building wealth and instead take actionable steps towards financial security and success.

WAITING TOO LONG TO INVEST —

Once you've established a healthy savings account, the next step is to consider investing your money to make it work for you. Diversifying your investments is key, as it allows you to spread your risk across different assets and strategies, whether they are high-risk or low-risk options. Leaving your money sitting in a bank account is not ideal, as inflation can erode its value over time, resulting in a loss of purchasing power.

Many people find reasons to delay investing, citing factors such as lack of time or uncertainty about where to start. However, the longer you wait to begin investing, the harder it becomes to achieve your financial goals. Time is a crucial factor in investing, as it allows your investments to grow and compound over time. Those who start investing early have the advantage of time on their side, enabling them to potentially achieve greater returns compared to those who delay getting started.

By investing early and regularly, you can take advantage of compounding returns, where your initial investment earns returns, which are then reinvested to generate even more returns over time. This can significantly accelerate the growth of your wealth and help you achieve your financial objectives more efficiently. Don't let hesitation or uncertainty hold you back from investing—take action now to secure your financial future and unlock the power of compound growth.

In the journey towards financial freedom and wealth building, finding the right approach and tools that resonate with you is crucial. Whether you are approaching investment from an employee or entrepreneur perspective, or you prefer high-risk or low-risk strategies, there are options available to match your investing style.

It's essential to explore different avenues and resources to identify what works best for you. This could involve seeking guidance from financial advisors, researching investment platforms, or attending workshops and seminars to enhance your knowledge and skills in investing.

Remember that there is no one-size-fits-all approach to investing. What works for one person may not necessarily work for another. By exploring various investment opportunities and understanding your own risk tolerance and financial goals, you can tailor your investment strategy to suit your individual preferences and circumstances.

The key is to remain proactive and open-minded in your approach to investing. Stay informed, continue learning, and be willing to adapt your strategy as needed to maximize your chances of success in achieving your financial objectives. With the right mindset and approach, you can take control of your financial future and build the wealth and security you desire.

NOTES:

____

____

____

____

CHAPTER 6

JENNIFER NICOLE LEE

STRENGTH TRAINING FOR LIFE: BUILDING MUSCLES AND RESILIENCE

You are an athlete, and in order to truly step into your new identity, we must explore the transformative power of strength training, not just for building muscles, but also for cultivating resilience in every aspect of life.

I'm thrilled to embark on this journey with you, where we'll explore the principles and practices of strength training that have the power to unlock your full potential. Strength training is not just about building muscles; it's about cultivating strength, resilience, and confidence in every aspect of your life.

Throughout this chapter, we'll discuss the fundamental principles of strength training, from proper form and technique to progressive overload and periodization. We'll uncover the science behind muscle growth and adaptation, empowering you with the knowledge and tools to design effective workouts tailored to your goals and abilities.

But strength training is more than just physical; it's a mindset—a commitment to pushing past limits, embracing challenges, and continuously striving for improvement. As we navigate through various strength training workouts and strategies, I'll be here to guide you every step of the way, offering support, motivation, and encouragement to help you stay focused and committed to your goals.

Together, we'll discover the transformative power of strength training, not only in sculpting your physique but also in building mental toughness, resilience, and self-confidence. Whether you're a beginner taking your first steps into the world of strength training or an experienced lifter looking to break through plateaus and reach new heights, I'm excited to be your guide on this journey toward unlocking your full potential.

Strength Training Workouts Suggestions

Whether you're a beginner looking to build a foundation of strength, an intermediate athlete seeking to progress to the next level, or an advanced lifter aiming for peak performance, there's a strength training workout routine that's right for you. Let's explore sample workouts tailored to each level:

Beginner Workout:

For beginners, it's essential to start with foundational movements and focus on mastering proper form and technique before progressing to heavier weights. This beginner strength training workout is designed to introduce you to key exercises while emphasizing quality over quantity:

Squats: 3 sets of 8-10 repetitions

- Stand with feet hip-width apart, toes slightly turned out.
- Lower your body by bending your knees and hips, keeping your chest up and back straight.
- Lower until your thighs are parallel to the ground, then push through your heels to return to the starting position.

Push-ups (or modified push-ups):
3 sets of 8-10 repetitions

- Start in a plank position with hands slightly wider than shoulder-width apart.
- Lower your body by bending your elbows until your chest nearly touches the ground.
- Push through your palms to return to the starting position.

Dumbbell Rows: 3 sets of 8-10 repetitions per arm

- Hold a dumbbell in one hand and place the opposite knee and hand on a bench.

- Keeping your back flat, pull the dumbbell towards your hip, squeezing your shoulder blades together.
- Lower the weight with control and repeat on the other side.

Lunges: 3 sets of 8-10 repetitions per leg

- Stand tall with feet hip-width apart.
- Step forward with one foot, lowering your body until both knees are bent at a 90-degree angle.
- Push through your front heel to return to the starting position.
- Alternate legs for each repetition.

Plank: 3 sets, holding for 30-60 seconds

- Start in a plank position with elbows directly beneath shoulders and body in a straight line from head to heels.
- Engage your core and hold the position, focusing on keeping your body stable and avoiding sagging or arching.

Perform each exercise with controlled movements, focusing on proper form and technique. Begin with lighter weights or bodyweight and gradually increase the intensity as you become more comfortable with the exercises. Remember to rest for 1-2 minutes between sets to allow for recovery.

This beginner workout routine will help you build a solid foundation of strength while minimizing the risk of injury. As you progress, you can gradually increase the weight, repetitions, or difficulty of exercises to continue challenging your muscles and advancing your fitness level.

Intermediate Workout:

As an intermediate lifter, you've already built a solid foundation of strength and mastered the basics of strength training. Now, it's time to increase the intensity and challenge your muscles in new ways to continue stimulating growth and progress. Here's a sample intermediate strength training workout designed to push your limits and take your fitness to the next level:

Barbell Back Squats: 4 sets of 6-8 repetitions

- Set up a barbell on a squat rack at about shoulder height.
- Step under the barbell and position it across your upper back, resting on your traps.
- Step back from the rack and stand with your feet shoulder-width apart.

- Keeping your chest up and back straight, lower your body by bending your knees and hips until your thighs are parallel to the ground.

- Push through your heels to return to the starting position, squeezing your glutes at the top.

Bench Press: 4 sets of 6-8 repetitions

- Lie flat on a bench with your feet planted firmly on the ground.

- Grip the barbell slightly wider than shoulder-width apart and lower it to your chest, keeping your elbows tucked.

- Push the barbell back up to the starting position, fully extending your arms without locking out your elbows.

Deadlifts: 4 sets of 6-8 repetitions

- Stand with your feet hip-width apart, toes under the barbell.

- Bend at your hips and knees to lower your body and grasp the barbell with an overhand grip, hands slightly wider than shoulder-width apart.

- Keep your back flat, chest up, and shoulders back as you lift the barbell by driving through your heels and extending your hips and knees.

- Lower the barbell back to the ground with control, maintaining a flat back throughout the movement.

Pull-ups (or assisted pull-ups): 4 sets of 6-8 repetitions

- Grip an overhead bar with your hands slightly wider than shoulder-width apart, palms facing away from you.

- Engage your back muscles and pull your body up until your chin clears the bar.

- Lower your body back down with control until your arms are fully extended.

Romanian Deadlifts: 4 sets of 6-8 repetitions

- Hold a barbell with an overhand grip, hands shoulder-width apart, and stand with your feet hip-width apart.

- Keeping your back flat and chest up, hinge at your hips and lower the barbell towards the ground while maintaining a slight bend in your knees.

- Lower the barbell until you feel a stretch in your hamstrings, then return to the starting position by driving through your heels and extending your hips.

Focus on progressively overloading your muscles by increasing the weight or resistance used in each exercise while maintaining proper form and technique. Rest for 1-2 minutes between sets to allow for adequate recovery.

Advanced Workout:

As an advanced lifter, you're ready to push your limits and take your strength training to the next level. Here's a sample advanced strength training workout designed to challenge your muscles and stimulate maximal muscle growth:

Barbell Squats: 5 sets of 4-6 repetitions

- Load a barbell with an appropriate weight and position it across your upper back.
- Perform squats with proper form, focusing on depth, control, and explosiveness.

Weighted Dips: 5 sets of 4-6 repetitions

- Set up parallel bars at shoulder width apart.
- Hold onto the bars and lift yourself up, slowly lower yourself down, then push back up explosively.

Barbell Rows: 5 sets of 4-6 repetitions

- Hold a barbell with an overhand grip, hands slightly wider than shoulder-width apart.
- Bend your knees slightly and hinge at the hips, keeping your back flat and chest up.

- Pull the barbell towards your lower chest, squeezing your shoulder blades together, then lower the barbell back to the starting position with control.

Power Cleans: 5 sets of 4-6 repetitions

- Start with a barbell on the ground, squat down and grasp it with an overhand grip slightly wider than shoulder width.
- Explosively extend your hips, knees, and ankles while shrugging your shoulders and pulling the barbell up.
- Drop into a front squat position, catching the barbell on your shoulders, then stand up to complete the movement.

Overhead Press: 5 sets of 4-6 repetitions

- Set up a barbell at shoulder height on a squat rack.
- Grip the barbell with your hands slightly wider than shoulder-width apart and press it overhead until your arms are fully extended.
- Lower the barbell back to the starting position with control.

Incorporate advanced techniques such as supersets, drop sets, and rest-pause sets to maximize muscle stimulation and adaptation. Remember to focus on proper form and technique, and listen to your body to avoid overtraining and injury. Rest for 2-3 minutes between sets to allow for maximal recovery.

By progressively challenging your muscles with these advanced strength training workouts, you can continue to stimulate growth and push your limits, ultimately achieving your fitness goals and reaching peak performance.

Importance of Recovery

While strength training is essential for building muscles and improving performance, adequate recovery is equally crucial for preventing injury and maximizing results. Here's why prioritizing recovery is essential and how you can implement effective recovery strategies into your routine:

Sports Massage:

Regular sports massages can provide numerous benefits for recovery and overall muscle health. These massages can help reduce muscle tension, improve circulation, and promote relaxation, which aids in reducing muscle soreness and enhancing recovery. Additionally, sports massage can target specific areas of tightness or discomfort, helping to alleviate muscle imbalances and prevent injuries.

Chiropractic Care:

Chiropractic adjustments are another valuable tool for enhancing recovery and optimizing performance. By improving joint mobility, alleviating pain, and optimizing nervous system function, chiropractic care can enhance movement quality and overall performance. Regular chiropractic adjustments can help address any biomechanical imbalances or restrictions, allowing you to move more efficiently and effectively during workouts.

Trigger Point Release:

Self-myofascial release techniques, such as foam rolling and using massage balls, are effective for releasing tight muscles, improving flexibility, and reducing the risk of injury. By targeting trigger points or knots in the muscles, these techniques help improve blood flow and oxygenation to the muscles, promoting faster recovery and reducing muscle soreness. Incorporating self-myofascial release into your post-workout routine can help speed up recovery and enhance overall muscle health.

Epsom Salt Baths:

Soaking in an Epsom salt bath is a simple yet effective way to promote relaxation and aid in muscle recovery. Epsom salt contains magnesium sulfate, which has been shown to help relax muscles, reduce inflammation, and alleviate soreness. Taking a warm Epsom salt bath after intense workouts can help soothe tired muscles, promote recovery, and reduce the risk of delayed onset muscle soreness (DOMS).

By incorporating these recovery strategies into your routine, you can optimize your recovery, reduce the risk of injury, and bounce back stronger and more resilient for your next workout. Remember, recovery is an essential part of the training process, so prioritize rest and recovery just as much as you do your workouts. Incorporating these recovery strategies into your routine will help ensure that you're giving your body the support it needs to perform at its best and achieve your fitness goals safely and effectively.

NOTES:

CHAPTER 7

ALKA SHARMA

NAVIGATING MARKET VOLATILITY: FINANCIAL STRATEGIES FOR STABILITY AND BUDGETING STRATEGIES FOR REAL ESTATE VENTURES

Diversifying your investment portfolio is a fundamental principle in the world of finance, and it's one that cannot be overstated. The concept revolves around spreading your investments across a range of different asset classes, industries, geographic regions, and investment vehicles. The aim is to minimize risk exposure and optimize potential returns.

One of the key reasons for diversification is risk management. By investing in a variety of assets, you reduce the impact of any single investment's poor performance on your overall portfolio. For example, if you have all your investments in one industry and that industry experiences a downturn, your entire portfolio could suffer significant losses. Diversification helps mitigate this risk by spreading your investments across different sectors, such as technology, healthcare, and consumer goods, among others.

Moreover, diversification can also enhance potential returns. While some investments may perform poorly, others may perform well, offsetting losses and potentially increasing overall portfolio returns. Different asset classes have different risk-return profiles, and by diversifying, you can capture opportunities for growth while minimizing downside risk.

Staying disciplined with investment decisions is another critical aspect of portfolio management. It involves adhering to your investment strategy and objectives, regardless of short-term market fluctuations or emotional impulses. Discipline helps you avoid making impulsive decisions based on fear or greed, which can lead to suboptimal outcomes.

Discipline also entails regularly reviewing and rebalancing your portfolio to ensure it remains aligned with your long-term goals and risk tolerance. This may involve selling investments that have become overweighted or underperforming and reallocating funds to assets that offer better prospects.

Diversification and discipline go hand in hand in building a resilient and successful investment portfolio. By spreading your investments strategically and adhering to a disciplined approach, you can better navigate market volatility, reduce risk, and position yourself for long-term financial success.

Price swings in the financial markets can indeed be exhilarating for investors, presenting opportunities for profit as well as challenges. However, it's crucial for investors to approach these fluctuations with a level-headed mindset and employ informed decision-making and risk management techniques.

Firstly, informed decision-making involves conducting thorough research and analysis before making investment decisions. This includes studying market trends, analyzing company financials, and understanding the broader economic environment. By staying informed about the factors influencing asset prices, investors can make more educated decisions and better anticipate potential market movements.

Additionally, risk management techniques are essential for mitigating the impact of price swings on investment portfolios. This can involve strategies such as diversification, where investors spread their investments across different asset classes to reduce overall risk exposure. Diversification helps cushion against losses in one area of the portfolio by offsetting them with gains in other areas.

Furthermore, setting clear investment goals and maintaining a disciplined approach can help investors navigate price swings more effectively. Having a well-defined investment strategy and sticking to it, even in the face of market volatility, can prevent impulsive decision-making driven by emotions such as fear or greed.

Below are strategies to implement in building your portfolio:

Diversification is indeed a fundamental principle in managing investment risk effectively. By spreading investments across different asset classes and sectors, such as healthcare, technology, and utilities, investors can reduce their exposure to the fluctuations of any single investment or market segment.

One key benefit of diversification is its ability to act as a protective shield during volatile market conditions. When one area of the portfolio experiences losses, gains in other areas can help offset these losses, thereby helping to stabilize overall portfolio performance.

When implementing diversification strategies, it's important for investors to consider their risk tolerance levels. This involves assessing how comfortable they are with taking on risk in pursuit of potential returns. For instance, some investors may have a higher risk tolerance and be willing to accept greater volatility in exchange for the possibility of higher returns. Others may prefer a more conservative approach, prioritizing capital preservation over aggressive growth.

Investing in stocks, for example, can offer varying levels of risk and return potential. Stocks of established companies in stable industries may offer lower risk but slower returns, while stocks of emerging companies or industries may carry higher risk but also the potential for higher returns. Understanding your risk tolerance can help guide your decisions when diversifying your investment portfolio, ensuring that it aligns with your financial goals and comfort level with risk.

Embracing a long-term investment approach can offer investors a sense of peace of mind and stability, particularly during periods of short-term market volatility. By focusing on long-term financial goals and investment strategies, investors can better weather the ups and downs of the market with confidence.

One of the key advantages of a long-term investment plan is its ability to provide a steady outlook that transcends short-term market fluctuations. Rather than reacting impulsively to market movements, long-term investors maintain a steadfast commitment to their financial objectives, knowing that short-term fluctuations are often just temporary blips on the radar.

Implementing a long-term investment strategy involves aligning investment decisions with broader financial goals, such as retirement planning, wealth accumulation, or funding education expenses. By maintaining a disciplined approach to investing over the long term, investors can cultivate a sense of stability amidst market volatility, allowing them to stay focused on their objectives even during turbulent times.

While it's natural for markets to experience fluctuations and downturns periodically, a long-term perspective reminds investors of the historical resilience of the market. Over time, markets have demonstrated a remarkable ability to recover and grow, rewarding patient and resilient investors who stay the course during challenging periods.

Ultimately, adopting a long-term investment mindset offers investors the peace of mind and confidence needed to navigate the inevitable twists and turns of the market, knowing that they are positioned for success over the long haul.

The use of stress testing in investments involves licensed financial advisors setting up scenarios to test portfolios under various market conditions. These stress tests provide valuable insights into how investments perform during different market scenarios. By conducting stress tests, advisors can offer insights into the performance of investments under different conditions, enabling investors to make informed decisions and adjustments before volatility strikes. This proactive approach allows investors to navigate market fluctuations more effectively and optimize their investment strategies for long-term success.

ASSET ALLOCATION —

Asset allocation is a crucial strategy that should be tailored to your risk tolerance and financial goals. Whether you aim for high risk or low, your asset allocation should reflect this. Personally, I prefer a medium to low-risk approach, particularly in sectors like energy and utilities. This provides a buffer against market fluctuations while still allowing for potential growth. It's essential to assess your risk tolerance and investment preferences. If you're unsure, consulting with a wealth management advisor can help you make informed decisions and create the right investment strategy for your needs.

The Golden Rule of Investing:

The Golden Rule of investing emphasizes the importance of maintaining a rational and disciplined approach, especially during times of market volatility. Emotions such as fear, greed, or panic can cloud judgment and lead to impulsive decisions that may harm your investment portfolio in the long run.

By adhering to this rule, investors can avoid making reactionary moves based on short-term fluctuations in the market. Instead, they should stay focused on their long-term investment goals and adhere to their predetermined investment strategy.

Maintaining a rational mindset allows investors to make informed decisions based on careful analysis and consideration of market conditions. It helps to avoid the pitfalls of emotional investing, which often result in buying high and selling low, contrary to sound investment principles.

Ultimately, the Golden Rule reminds investors to approach investing with patience, discipline, and a long-term perspective, thereby maximizing the potential for success and wealth accumulation over time.

Market volatility refers to the rapid and unpredictable changes in the prices of assets within financial markets. While it can be unsettling for investors, it's important to recognize that volatility is a natural part of the financial landscape and can present both opportunities and challenges.

During periods of market volatility, it's crucial for investors to maintain a clear end goal in mind. This could be achieving long-term financial stability, funding retirement, or reaching a certain level of wealth. By anchoring investment decisions to this end goal, investors can avoid being swayed by short-term market fluctuations and remain focused on their broader objectives.

Discipline is another key aspect of navigating market volatility successfully. This involves sticking to a well-thought-out investment strategy even when faced with market uncertainty. Rather than making impulsive decisions based on fear or speculation, disciplined investors adhere to their predetermined asset allocation and risk tolerance levels.

Safeguarding for the future is also essential in times of market volatility. This includes diversifying investment portfolios across different asset classes, industries, and geographic regions to reduce overall risk exposure. Additionally, investors may consider incorporating defensive strategies, such as holding cash reserves or investing in assets that tend to perform well during market downturns.

Ultimately, adopting a well-rounded approach to mitigate risk can help investors navigate market volatility with confidence. By staying focused on long-term goals, maintaining discipline in investment decisions, and implementing prudent risk management strategies, investors can better weather periods of market turbulence and position themselves for success in the long run.

Financial planning: a step-by-step guide.

This is a crucial juncture in your life. Financial planning involves assessing your current financial situation and creating a plan to reach both short and long-term goals.

Let's take a look at what a financial plan entails.

It's a comprehensive picture of your current finances, financial goals, and the strategies you've set to achieve these goals. Developing good financial habits and planning should include managing cash flow, savings, debt, investments, and any other elements of your financial life.

Financial planning is an ongoing process that provides a comprehensive view of your entire financial situation, enabling you to create strategies for achieving both short and long-term goals. Seeking advice from professionals like financial advisors can help reduce stress for individuals when it comes to allocating money and managing finances. This, in turn, assists in building a nest egg or cushion for the bigger picture, such as retirement.

Creating a financial plan is crucial for maximizing the potential of your assets, whether it's real estate, stocks, or shares. It gives you the confidence to hold onto your investments, even during challenging times.

Set Financial Goals:

Begin by defining your financial objectives. Whether it's buying a house, retiring early, or paying off debts, having clear goals will guide your savings and investment decisions.

Track Your Money:

Understand your cash flow by tracking your income and expenses. This provides an accurate picture of your financial situation and helps in setting short, medium, and long-term goals.

Budget for Emergencies:

Allocate funds for unexpected expenses and emergencies. Start with small amounts and gradually increase to cover at least one month of basic living expenses.

Tackle High-Interest Debt:

Prioritize paying off high-interest debts such as credit cards and loans. Minimize interest payments by paying more than the minimum amount due.

Plan for Retirement:

Take advantage of employer-sponsored retirement plans like a 401(k) and contribute enough to receive employer matching, if available. Gradually increase contributions over time.

Optimize Your Finances and Tax Planning:

Maximize tax benefits and credits by understanding available deductions and credits. Avoid common pitfalls and plan ahead to minimize tax liabilities.

Investing to Build Future Goals:

Investing is not just for the wealthy. Start investing early, even with small amounts, to benefit from compounding growth over time.

Grow in Financial Well-Being:

Prioritize contributions to retirement accounts, build emergency funds, and secure insurance coverage to protect against financial setbacks.

Estate Planning: Protecting Your Financial Well-Being:

Ensure your assets are distributed according to your wishes by creating a will and planning for the future needs of your loved ones.

By following these steps, you'll create a comprehensive financial plan that safeguards your financial future and helps you achieve your goals.

Financial planning provides a guiding framework for managing your finances. It's an ongoing process that involves assessing your entire financial situation to develop strategies for achieving both short-term and long-term goals.

NOTES:

____

____

____

____

____

____

____

____

____

____

____

____

____

____

CHAPTER 8

JENNIFER NICOLE LEE

CARDIOVASCULAR HEALTH: THE KEY TO ENDURANCE AND VITALITY

In this chapter, we take a deep dive into the realm of cardiovascular health—a cornerstone of endurance, vitality, and overall well-being. I invite you to join me as we explore the critical role that cardiovascular fitness plays in shaping our physical and mental resilience.

Your cardiovascular system serves as the engine of your body, tirelessly pumping blood, oxygen, and nutrients to every cell, tissue, and organ. It is the foundation upon which your endurance and vitality are built, supporting your capacity for sustained physical activity and fueling your journey toward peak performance.

In the pages ahead, we'll uncover the profound benefits of cardiovascular exercise, from strengthening your heart and lowering blood pressure to boosting your mood and improving sleep quality. We'll discuss practical strategies for enhancing your cardiovascular health, empowering you to take control of your fitness journey and unlock your full potential.

Whether you're a seasoned athlete striving for peak performance or someone looking to prioritize their health and well-being, this chapter is for you. Together, we'll discover the transformative power of cardiovascular health and learn how to harness its energy to propel us toward our goals.

So, lace up your shoes, take a deep breath, and let's level up our cardiovascular vitality—a journey that promises not only physical strength and endurance but also a renewed sense of vitality and zest for life. Welcome to the world of cardiovascular health—where every beat of your heart is a testament to your strength, resilience, and unwavering determination to thrive.

The Benefits of Cardiovascular Exercise

Regular cardiovascular exercise offers a multitude of benefits that positively impact both your physical and mental health. Let's delve deeper into some of the key benefits:

Improved Heart Health:

Cardiovascular exercise serves as a potent stimulant for your heart, strengthening its muscle fibers, enhancing its efficiency, and promoting optimal blood circulation throughout your body. Through regular aerobic activity, such as running, cycling, or swimming, you can significantly reduce the risk of cardiovascular diseases such as heart disease and stroke. By challenging your cardiovascular system, you encourage it to adapt and become more resilient, leading to a healthier heart that can better withstand the demands of everyday life.

Enhanced Endurance:

Engaging in cardiovascular exercise trains your body to efficiently deliver oxygen to your muscles, allowing them to perform at their peak for longer durations. As you consistently challenge your cardiovascular system with activities like jogging, brisk walking, or hiking, your body becomes more adept at utilizing oxygen and energy sources, resulting in increased endurance and stamina. Whether you're chasing after your children, tackling household chores, or conquering a challenging hike, improved endurance enables you to tackle daily tasks with ease and confidence.

Weight Management:

Cardiovascular exercise is a powerful tool for managing body weight and promoting fat loss. By engaging in activities that elevate your heart rate and increase calorie expenditure, such as running, cycling, or dancing, you can create a calorie deficit that contributes to weight loss over time. Additionally, regular cardiovascular exercise helps boost your metabolism, making it easier to maintain a healthy weight and body composition. Whether your goal is to shed a few pounds or maintain your current weight, incorporating cardiovascular exercise into your routine can help you achieve and sustain your desired results.

Reduced Stress and Anxiety:

Cardiovascular exercise has profound effects on your mental well-being, helping to alleviate stress, anxiety, and tension. When you engage in aerobic activities, your body releases endorphins, neurotransmitters that act as natural mood lifters and stress relievers. These feel-good chemicals flood your brain, promoting feelings of relaxation, happiness, and overall well-being. Whether you're jogging through the park, cycling along a scenic trail, or dancing to your favorite music, cardiovascular exercise provides a powerful outlet for releasing pent-up stress and tension, leaving you feeling refreshed, rejuvenated, and ready to tackle whatever challenges come your way.

Better Sleep:

Regular cardiovascular exercise can have a significant impact on your sleep quality and duration, leading to more restful and rejuvenating nights. By engaging in aerobic activities during the day, you expend excess energy, reduce feelings of restlessness, and promote relaxation, making it easier to fall asleep and stay asleep throughout the night. Additionally, the release of endorphins during exercise can help regulate your body's sleep-wake cycle, leading to more consistent sleep patterns and improved overall sleep quality. Whether you prefer morning runs, afternoon swims, or evening walks, incorporating cardiovascular exercise into your daily routine can help you enjoy deeper, more restorative sleep and wake up feeling refreshed and energized each morning.

In summary, the benefits of cardiovascular exercise extend far beyond physical fitness, encompassing improvements in heart health, endurance, weight management, stress reduction, and sleep quality. By making regular aerobic activity a priority in your life, you can enjoy a multitude of health benefits that enhance both your physical and mental well-being, allowing you to live life to the fullest with vitality, energy, and resilience.

Practical Strategies for Improving Cardiovascular Health

Incorporating cardiovascular exercise into your routine is essential for maintaining optimal cardiovascular health. Here are some practical strategies to help you improve and maintain your cardiovascular fitness:

Choose Activities You Enjoy:

Finding activities that you genuinely enjoy is key to sticking with your cardiovascular exercise routine in the long term. Whether it's running, cycling, swimming, dancing, or hiking, discovering activities that resonate with you and fit into your lifestyle will make it easier to stay consistent and motivated. Experiment with different types of activities until you find ones that bring you joy and fulfillment, and don't be afraid to step outside of your comfort zone to try new things.

Start Slowly and Progress Gradually:

If you're new to exercise or returning after a break, it's essential to start slowly and gradually increase the duration and intensity of your workouts. Rushing into intense exercise without allowing your body time to adapt can increase the risk of injury and burnout. Listen to your body and pay attention to any signs of discomfort or fatigue, and don't push yourself too hard, too soon. Begin with shorter, low-intensity workouts and gradually build up your endurance and stamina over time.

Aim for Regular Exercise:

Consistency is key when it comes to improving and maintaining cardiovascular fitness. Aim for at least 150 minutes of moderate-intensity cardiovascular exercise per week, or 75 minutes of vigorous-intensity exercise, spread out over several days. Incorporating regular exercise into your routine helps establish healthy habits and ensures that you're consistently challenging your cardiovascular system to adapt and improve. Schedule your workouts at times that work best for you, whether it's first thing in the morning, during your lunch break, or in the evening after work, and prioritize them just like you would any other important appointment.

Include Variety in Your Workouts:

Mixing up your cardiovascular workouts is essential for preventing boredom, plateauing, and overuse injuries. Incorporate a variety of activities, intensities, and durations into your routine to challenge your body in different ways and keep your workouts exciting. Try alternating between different forms of cardiovascular exercise, such as running, cycling, swimming, or group fitness classes, to work different muscle groups and keep your workouts fresh and engaging. Additionally, vary the intensity and duration of your workouts to continually challenge your cardiovascular system and promote ongoing improvements in fitness.

Monitor Your Progress:

Keeping track of your workouts and progress is essential for staying motivated and on track toward your fitness goals. Keep a workout journal or use a fitness tracking app to record the duration, intensity, and type of exercise performed during each workout, as well as any other relevant information, such as heart rate, distance covered, or calories burned. Monitoring your progress allows you to set realistic goals, track improvements over time, and identify areas where you may need to adjust your training program. Celebrate your successes along the way, whether it's reaching a new distance milestone, improving your pace, or simply sticking with your exercise routine consistently.

By incorporating these practical strategies into your routine, you can improve and maintain your cardiovascular health, boost your fitness levels, and enjoy the numerous benefits that come with regular exercise. Remember to listen to your body, prioritize consistency, and have fun exploring different activities and workouts to find what works best for you. With dedication, determination, and a positive mindset, you can achieve your cardiovascular fitness goals and live a happier, healthier life.

Optimizing your cardiovascular health is crucial for achieving endurance, vitality, and overall well-being. Your cardiovascular system serves as the foundation of your body's ability to function efficiently, delivering oxygen and nutrients to your muscles and organs while removing waste products. By prioritizing your cardiovascular health and incorporating regular exercise into your routine, you can reap numerous benefits that extend far beyond physical fitness.

Regular cardiovascular exercise plays a pivotal role in enhancing your cardiovascular fitness, which refers to the efficiency and effectiveness of your heart and lungs in delivering oxygen to your muscles during physical activity. By engaging in activities such as running, cycling, swimming, or brisk walking, you can strengthen your heart muscle, improve circulation, and enhance your body's ability to utilize oxygen, leading to increased endurance and stamina.

In addition to improving your physical fitness, regular cardiovascular exercise can also reduce the risk of chronic diseases such as heart disease, stroke, type 2 diabetes, and certain cancers. By maintaining a healthy weight, lowering blood pressure and cholesterol levels, and improving insulin sensitivity, cardiovascular exercise helps protect against the development of these conditions and promotes overall cardiovascular health.

Furthermore, investing in your cardiovascular health is an investment in your future vitality and longevity. By adopting a consistent exercise routine and following practical strategies for improvement, you can not only enhance your current quality of life but also increase your chances of living a longer, healthier life. Regular exercise has been shown to improve mood, reduce stress and anxiety, enhance cognitive function, and promote better sleep—all of which contribute to overall well-being and longevity.

It's essential to remember that optimizing your cardiovascular health is not just about the physical benefits—it's also about cultivating a positive mindset and prioritizing self-care. By making exercise a regular part of your routine and embracing healthy lifestyle habits, you can enhance your cardiovascular fitness, reduce the risk of chronic disease, and improve your overall quality of life. So lace up your shoes, hit the pavement, and invest in your cardiovascular health today for a brighter, healthier tomorrow.

NOTES:

CHAPTER 9

ALKA SHARMA

DIVERSIFYING YOUR PORTFOLIO FOR FINANCIAL SECURITY AND GENERATING INCOME IN REAL ESTATE, MY BEST INSIDER TIPS AND STRATEGIES

"Big opportunities always
present when they do, seize upon"
-Alka Sharma

Investing in stocks can be a lucrative endeavor, but it's essential to acknowledge the inherent risks involved. While stocks can provide impressive returns over time, they are also subject to market fluctuations and volatility. However, despite these risks, patient investors who weather the ups and downs of the market often see their investments grow substantially.

Diversification is a fundamental strategy in managing risk when investing in stocks. By spreading your investment across different sectors, industries, and types of companies, you can mitigate the impact of adverse events affecting any single stock or sector. This approach helps to balance the potential upsides and downsides of individual investments, ultimately reducing overall portfolio risk.

While investing in stocks carries risks, the potential rewards can be significant. By maintaining a diversified portfolio and exercising patience, investors can navigate market uncertainties and work towards achieving their financial goals.

Outlined below are four reasons for maintaining a concentrated portfolio.

A concentrated portfolio typically consists of 20-30 securities or even fewer. In the context of equity mutual funds, it involves holding a limited number of stocks, providing higher exposure to individual companies.

Ownership of Businesses:

Stocks represent ownership stakes in businesses, not just pieces of paper with fluctuating prices. Understanding the fundamentals of the underlying businesses is crucial to avoid being swayed by short-term market fluctuations.

Risk Consideration:

While many investors associate risk with volatility, it's essential to view risk in terms of the likelihood of a permanent loss of investment capital due to the underlying performance of the business. Focusing on the fundamentals of the companies in your portfolio can help mitigate this risk.

Margin of Safety:

Investing in companies with a high margin of safety involves paying significantly less than the intrinsic value of the business. This approach ensures a greater probability of success in your investments by obtaining them at a discounted price relative to their true worth.

Tech Stock Consideration:

When considering tech stocks, it's prudent to exercise caution due to their shorter lifespan compared to non-technology stocks. Tech companies often face rapid changes in technology and market trends, making their stocks potentially riskier investments.

Diversifying your investments across a wide range of companies is like casting a net wide in the ocean. By spreading your investments, you reduce the risk of relying too heavily on the performance of any single company. If one company underperforms or faces challenges, the impact on your overall portfolio is minimized because you have other investments to help offset potential losses. This strategy helps to protect your investment capital and increase the likelihood of achieving your financial goals over the long term.

Example of concentrated stocks:

Consider a business owner who owns several businesses in their hometown, such as a McDonald's franchise, a car dealership, and rental properties. Despite having multiple businesses, would you say their wealth is diversified? Yes, indeed. Now, how are stocks any different?

Stocks represent ownership in a business. Researching stocks requires time and effort, as investors must sift through hundreds or thousands of companies to find those with strong fundamentals and reasonable prices. However, investors need not dedicate full-time hours to this task; even spending 5-10 hours per week on research can suffice. Alternatively, if time is limited, hiring a broker can provide valuable assistance, albeit at a cost for their services.

For those seeking a diversified investment option without the need for extensive research, investing in an S&P 500 index fund is highly recommended. This fund comprises the largest 500 companies on the stock exchange, offering exposure to a broad range of publicly traded companies. By investing in the index, investors effectively own a piece of each business included in the fund. As the portfolio grows, investors benefit from the collective performance of these companies, albeit with diminishing returns as the portfolio size increases.

Managing risks for financial security is crucial, especially knowing how to construct the perfect investment portfolio to weather economic downturns and be recession-proof.

What is an investment portfolio? It's essentially a basket of various investments designed to complement each other and enhance returns for the investor. A well-structured portfolio typically includes a mix of stocks, bonds, mutual funds, ETFs (exchange-traded funds), cryptocurrencies, commodities, and even alternative assets like art and watches.

Exchange-traded funds (ETFs) offer a convenient way to gain exposure to the overall market, especially in a recessionary environment. It's wise to allocate a higher percentage of your portfolio to sectors that typically perform well during economic downturns, such as utilities, consumer goods, and healthcare. These sectors tend to demonstrate resilience during challenging economic times, providing stability and potential growth opportunities for investors.

If your goal is broad diversification across a wide range of stocks but you don't want to individually invest in 50 or 100 different stocks, consider buying an ETF. ETFs offer a simple and efficient way to achieve diversification by allowing investors to own a basket of stocks within a single investment. Instead of having to select and manage numerous individual stocks, an ETF provides exposure to a diversified portfolio of assets, often tracking an index or specific sector.

By investing in an ETF, you can spread your risk across multiple companies and sectors without the need for extensive research and monitoring. This approach can help mitigate the impact of poor performance from any single stock while still allowing you to participate in the overall growth potential of the market. Additionally, ETFs typically have lower fees and expenses compared to actively managed funds, making them a cost-effective option for achieving diversification in your investment portfolio.

The goal here is to create a well-balanced investment portfolio that diversifies investments, thereby reducing risks during market cycles and enhancing overall returns. Diversification involves spreading investments across various asset classes, industries, and geographic regions to minimize the impact of any single investment's performance on the portfolio as a whole. By diversifying, investors aim to achieve a more stable and consistent investment performance over time, regardless of market conditions.

Diversifying your portfolio with mixed assets involves spreading your investments across different types of assets, such as stocks, bonds, real estate, and commodities. This strategy allows you to benefit from the gains of one asset class while others may experience declines in value. For example, during periods of economic growth, stocks may perform well, while during economic downturns, bonds or real estate may offer stability and potential returns. By holding a mix of assets, you can reduce the overall risk in your portfolio and increase the likelihood of achieving your investment goals over the long term.

As an investor, it is crucial to understand your investment goals, risk tolerance, and time horizon. Paying careful attention to these factors and regularly reviewing your investment performances can help you make informed decisions and stay on track to achieve your financial objectives.

Another important consideration is when you'll need access to your invested funds. It's advisable to keep the money in the markets for a maximum of 2-3 years. Essentially, you should have a clear plan for your funds, especially in scenarios like a recession or during bear markets. This ensures that your investment strategy aligns with your financial goals and timeline, minimizing the risk of being caught off guard by market downturns.

A bear market is characterized by a downturn in the market, often instilling fear in investors. These downturns are an inevitable part of market cycles, but they also present opportunities for savvy investors. Bear markets typically have relatively short cycles, during which stocks across the board show signs of decline. However, despite the initial apprehension they may cause, bear markets can offer attractive investment opportunities for those who are prepared to capitalize on them.

Here are three investment strategies:

INCOME PORTFOLIO:

An income portfolio involves investing in dividend-paying stocks and coupon-yielding bonds. Dividend-paying stocks are shares of companies that distribute a portion of their profits to shareholders regularly. Coupon-yielding bonds provide fixed interest payments over the bond's lifespan. As an investor, it's important to assess your risk tolerance and choose investments that align with your comfort level. Income portfolios typically include short to mid-term investments and require a clear understanding of your expected time horizon.

BALANCED PORTFOLIO:

A balanced portfolio combines investments in both bonds and stocks to reduce potential volatility. Investors seeking a balanced portfolio prioritize stability over high growth, accepting short-term fluctuations in exchange for smoother long-term returns.

GROWTH PORTFOLIO:

A growth portfolio focuses on investing in stocks expected to appreciate in value over time. This strategy is suitable for investors with a high tolerance for risk and a long time horizon. By selecting companies with strong growth potential, investors aim to maximize returns over the long term.

Implementing a hybrid approach to investments, whether in a recession or not, allows investors to optimize their strategies and maximize their potential returns.

Bear markets, characterized by widespread declines in stock prices and negative investor sentiment, can indeed present significant opportunities for investors. However, to take advantage of these opportunities, it's essential to be financially prepared.

Firstly, investors should prioritize building an emergency fund before considering investing in a bear market. This emergency fund should ideally cover at least six months of living expenses and be held in cash or highly liquid assets. By having this financial cushion, investors can weather any unexpected expenses or income disruptions without having to dip into their investment portfolio during volatile market conditions.

Keeping the emergency fund in a separate savings account ensures that it remains easily accessible when needed while also providing a degree of psychological comfort and financial security. This separation helps investors avoid the temptation to use these funds for non-emergency purposes and reinforces the importance of maintaining a strong financial safety net.

Overall, while bear markets offer unique opportunities for long-term investors to capitalize on undervalued assets and potentially generate significant returns, ensuring financial stability through an emergency fund is a crucial first step in navigating these market downturns with confidence and resilience.

Everyone has their own set of goals they want to achieve through investing. By researching stocks and utilizing the resources available to you, you can begin to build your own investment portfolio and develop your investment strategies.

One effective way to characterize your investments is by allocating a portion of your income. For example, allocating 20% of your income to bonds and income stocks can provide a steady stream of income and serve as a hedge against market volatility. Bonds, in particular, are known for providing interest payments, which are backed by the government.

Income stocks, on the other hand, are stocks that consistently pay dividends to their shareholders. Dividends are regular payments made by companies, typically on a quarterly basis, to their shareholders as a share of the company's profits.

I have a rule when investing: I focus on companies that offer great returns and consult with a wealth management team to make informed decisions.

It's important to know your investment goals. Another 20% of your investment allocation can be directed towards growth stocks. These stocks are expected to have higher-than-average growth rates compared to the market as a whole. While growth stocks may underperform during recessions due to investor risk aversion, they have historically provided strong returns over the long term.

A further 20% of your investments can be allocated towards blue-chip stocks. These stocks belong to large, well-established companies with a proven track record of stability and reliable dividends. Examples include companies like Amazon, Google, and Facebook, which are widely recognized and used in our daily lives. Many investors consider blue-chip stocks to be a safer, more conservative investment option.

The remaining 10% of your investment allocation can be directed towards cryptocurrency. While I personally don't invest heavily in cryptocurrency due to its volatility, it can be a valuable investment during a recession. However, it's important to note that cryptocurrency is a higher-risk asset class, which is why I allocate a smaller portion of my portfolio to it.

In conclusion, making sound investment decisions requires careful consideration of various factors, including your risk tolerance, investment goals, and market conditions. By assessing your tolerance against market fluctuations, you can position yourself to achieve the best possible returns on your investments.

It's important to recognize that investing involves risk, and there are no guarantees of success. However, by conducting thorough research, diversifying your portfolio, and staying informed about market trends, you can make informed decisions that align with your financial objectives.

Additionally, it's crucial to remain patient and disciplined, especially during times of market volatility. Avoid making impulsive decisions based on short-term fluctuations, and instead, focus on the long-term growth potential of your investments.

By staying informed, understanding your risk tolerance, and maintaining a disciplined approach to investing, you can increase your chances of achieving your financial goals and securing a more prosperous future.

NOTES:

____

____

____

____

____

____

____

____

____

____

____

____

____

CHAPTER 10

JENNIFER NICOLE LEE

FLEXIBILITY AND BALANCE: YOGA AND PILATES FOR MIND-BODY HARMONY

"Movement is Medicine"
-Jennifer Nicole Lee

In today's fast-paced world, where the pursuit of success often takes precedence, it's easy to overlook the essential components of our well-being: flexibility and balance. As a fitness expert with over 20 years of experience, I can be one of the first to attest that incorporating both flexibility and balance into my wellness program has helped me not only be physically fit, but also financially fit. How? When you are in balance, you are healthier, and rarely sick. Sick days can put you back on the success trajectory, especially in running your businesses! So let's get to stretching.

These two pillars of physical wellness are not only foundational to our overall fitness but also play a pivotal role in achieving mental equilibrium and fostering a holistic sense of health and wealth.

Flexibility is more than just the ability to touch your toes or perform a split; it's about adaptability and resilience in the face of life's challenges. Just as a flexible body can bend without breaking, a flexible mind can navigate obstacles with grace and ease. When we cultivate physical flexibility through practices like yoga and Pilates, we also cultivate a mindset that is open to change and capable of embracing new opportunities.

Similarly, balance is crucial for maintaining stability and harmony in both our bodies and our lives. In the physical realm, balance requires coordination and strength in equal measure, ensuring that we move through the world with poise and confidence. But balance goes beyond mere physicality; it extends to our mental and emotional well-being as well. When we find balance in our lives—balancing work and play, ambition and relaxation, effort and surrender—we experience a sense of wholeness and fulfillment that transcends material success.

Yoga and Pilates are ancient practices that offer a holistic approach to mind-body harmony, addressing both flexibility and balance in equal measure. Through a combination of breathwork, meditation, and physical movement, these disciplines teach us to cultivate awareness, presence, and self-compassion. They invite us to explore the interconnectedness of our physical, mental, and spiritual selves, guiding us toward a state of inner peace and well-being.

In the pages that follow, we will delve into the transformative power of yoga and Pilates, exploring their profound effects on our physical health, mental clarity, and emotional resilience. We will discover how these ancient practices can help us cultivate flexibility and balance in all aspects of our lives, empowering us to live with greater vitality, purpose, and joy.

So join us on this journey of self-discovery and self-improvement as we unlock the secrets of optimal health and wealth through the practice of yoga and Pilates. Together, let's explore the infinite possibilities that await us when we embrace flexibility and balance as the cornerstones of our well-being

Yoga, originating from ancient India, is a holistic practice that transcends the boundaries of mere physical exercise. Its essence lies in fostering a harmonious integration of the body, mind, and spirit—a union that holds the key to profound personal transformation and holistic well-being.

At its core, yoga is a profound philosophy—a way of life—that extends far beyond the confines of a yoga mat. It is a journey of self-discovery and self-realization, inviting practitioners to explore the depths of their inner landscape and uncover the innate wisdom that resides within. Through a combination of breathwork, meditation, and physical movement, yoga offers a multifaceted approach to achieving balance and inner harmony.

Breathwork, or pranayama, serves as the foundation of the yogic practice, acting as a bridge between the physical and the spiritual realms. Through conscious control and regulation of the breath, practitioners learn to harness the life force energy (prana) that animates their being, cultivating a sense of vitality and aliveness that permeates every aspect of their existence. Breathwork not only oxygenates the body and calms the mind but also serves as a powerful tool for accessing deeper states of consciousness and expanding awareness.

Meditation, another fundamental aspect of yoga, offers a pathway to inner peace and spiritual awakening. By cultivating mindfulness and presence through the practice of meditation, practitioners learn to quiet the incessant chatter of the mind and tap into the timeless realm of pure awareness. In the stillness of meditation, they discover a sanctuary of inner calm and tranquility—a space where they can reconnect with their true essence and experience a profound sense of wholeness and well-being.

Physical movement, expressed through the practice of yoga asanas (postures), is a means of aligning the body, mind, and spirit in perfect harmony. Each posture is a unique expression of the body's innate intelligence, inviting practitioners to explore the full range of their physical capabilities and unlock the latent potential that lies within. Through the cultivation of flexibility, strength, and balance, practitioners not only enhance their physical health and vitality but also awaken to a deeper sense of self-awareness and self-empowerment.

Whether you're a seasoned yogi or a beginner, the benefits of incorporating yoga into your daily routine are manifold. From improved physical fitness and mental clarity to enhanced emotional well-being and spiritual growth, yoga offers something for everyone, regardless of age, ability, or background. By embracing the transformative power of yoga, practitioners can embark on a journey of self-discovery and self-transformation that leads to greater health, happiness, and fulfillment in all areas of life.

Pilates, conceived by Joseph Pilates in the early 20th century, stands as a testament to the enduring power of innovation in the realm of physical fitness. Unlike yoga, which traces its origins back thousands of years, Pilates represents a more recent development—a modern system of exercise that embodies principles of strength, flexibility, and alignment tailored to meet the needs of the contemporary practitioner.

At its core, Pilates is a comprehensive approach to physical conditioning that focuses on cultivating core strength, enhancing flexibility, and optimizing postural alignment. Unlike traditional strength training methods, which often prioritize isolated muscle groups, Pilates takes a more holistic approach, targeting the body as a unified whole. Through a series of precise movements and controlled breathing patterns, practitioners learn to engage their deep core muscles—the powerhouse of the body—in a coordinated and efficient manner.

Central to the Pilates method is the concept of core stability—a foundation upon which all movement is built. By strengthening the muscles of the abdomen, pelvis, and lower back, Pilates practitioners develop a solid foundation of support that enables them to move with grace and ease in their daily activities. This emphasis on core strength not only improves functional movement patterns but also reduces the risk of injury by promoting proper biomechanics and alignment.

In addition to core strength, Pilates also places a strong emphasis on flexibility—a quality that is essential for maintaining joint health and preventing stiffness and discomfort. Through a series of dynamic stretches and fluid movements, practitioners learn to lengthen and elongate their muscles, increasing their range of motion and enhancing overall flexibility. This emphasis on flexibility not only improves athletic performance but also promotes a sense of ease and freedom in movement, allowing practitioners to move with greater fluidity and grace.

Moreover, Pilates is renowned for its ability to improve posture—an often overlooked aspect of physical fitness that plays a crucial role in overall health and well-being. By addressing muscular imbalances and postural deviations, Pilates helps to realign the body and restore balance to the musculoskeletal system. This emphasis on postural alignment not only reduces the risk of injury and chronic pain but also enhances body awareness and self-confidence, empowering practitioners to stand tall and move with confidence in their daily lives.

Pilates offers a unique approach to physical fitness that combines elements of strength, flexibility, and alignment to create a balanced body that moves with grace and ease. Whether you're a seasoned athlete or a novice practitioner, Pilates offers something for everyone, providing a safe and effective way to improve core strength, enhance flexibility, and optimize postural alignment. So, whether you're looking to improve your athletic performance, alleviate chronic pain, or simply enhance your overall well-being, Pilates stands ready to help you achieve your goals and unleash your full potential.

Combining the principles of yoga and Pilates offers a comprehensive approach to fitness that addresses the needs of both body and mind. Let's explore some key practices from each discipline:

- Breath Awareness: Both yoga and Pilates place a strong emphasis on conscious breathing. Deep, diaphragmatic breathing not only oxygenates the body but also calms the mind and reduces stress. Incorporate breath awareness into your practice by focusing on the inhale and exhale with each movement.

- Mindful Movement: In yoga, each posture is performed mindfully, with attention to alignment and sensation. Similarly, Pilates encourages precision and control in every movement. Practice mindful movement by paying attention to the quality of each action, rather than simply going through the motions.

- Flexibility Training: Yoga postures (asanas) are designed to stretch and lengthen the muscles, improving flexibility and range of motion. Pilates exercises also promote flexibility, particularly in the spine and joints. Include a variety of stretches and flexibility exercises in your routine to maintain suppleness and prevent injury.

- Strength Building: While yoga primarily focuses on flexibility, it also builds strength, particularly in the core, arms, and legs. Pilates, meanwhile, is renowned for its ability to tone and sculpt the entire body, with an emphasis on the core muscles. Incorporate strength-building exercises from both disciplines to develop balanced muscle strength and stability.

- Balance Enhancement: Yoga and Pilates both challenge balance and coordination through a variety of standing, seated, and prone positions. Practicing balancing poses improves proprioception (awareness of body position) and enhances stability. Include balance exercises in your routine to improve coordination and prevent falls.

- Mind-Body Connection: Perhaps the most significant benefit of yoga and Pilates is the cultivation of the mind-body connection. By tuning into the body's sensations and observing the fluctuations of the mind, practitioners develop greater self-awareness and inner harmony. Dedicate time to meditation and relaxation practices to deepen this connection and promote overall well-being.

Incorporating yoga and Pilates into your fitness routine can have profound effects on both your physical and mental health. By embracing the principles of flexibility and balance, you can create a harmonious union between body, mind, and spirit, paving the way for a successful path to financial and physical fitness.

The journey towards optimal health and wealth is a profound and ongoing process, one that unfolds gradually over time and requires dedication, commitment, and a willingness to embrace change. It is not a destination to be reached but rather a path to be walked—a journey of growth, transformation, and self-discovery that unfolds with each step we take.

By embracing the wisdom of yoga and Pilates, we open ourselves up to a world of possibilities—a world where the body, mind, and spirit are united in perfect harmony, and where every moment becomes an opportunity for growth and self-improvement. These ancient practices offer us a roadmap for living a life of balance, vitality, and abundance—a life that nourishes our bodies, enriches our minds, and empowers our spirits to soar.

Through the practice of yoga, we learn to cultivate mindfulness, presence, and self-awareness—qualities that are essential for navigating the complexities of modern life with grace and ease. By tuning into the wisdom of our bodies and connecting with the rhythm of our breath, we discover a profound sense of peace and tranquility that transcends the chaos of the external world. Yoga teaches us to listen to our inner voice, to honor our deepest truths, and to embrace the fullness of who we are.

Similarly, Pilates offers us a pathway to strength, flexibility, and alignment—a pathway that enables us to move through the world with confidence and grace. By engaging our core muscles and improving our posture, we develop a solid foundation of support that enables us to move with greater ease and efficiency. Pilates teaches us to move with intention, to align our bodies with precision, and to cultivate a sense of balance and equilibrium that extends far beyond the confines of the studio.

Together, yoga and Pilates offer us a comprehensive approach to health and well-being—one that addresses the needs of the body, mind, and spirit in equal measure. By incorporating these practices into our daily lives, we create a lifestyle that honors our physical, mental, and emotional needs—a lifestyle that nourishes us from the inside out and empowers us to live our best lives.

So, roll out your mat, take a deep breath, and embark on this journey of self-discovery and self-improvement. Embrace the wisdom of yoga and Pilates, and allow yourself to be guided by their transformative power. Trust in the process, and know that every step you take brings you closer to a life of greater health, wealth, and happiness. Namaste.

NOTES:

CHAPTER 11

ALKA SHARMA

REAL ESTATE INVESTING: BUILDING WEALTH THROUGH PROPERTY

When acquiring wealth in the manner affluent individuals do, it's crucial to recognize a common pitfall: excessive consumer spending. In the United States, a staggering 70% of the population falls into the category of consumer spenders. Many individuals habitually spend money on items they don't truly need, often driven by the desire to impress others. Consequently, they may find themselves maxing out credit cards, and unless their financial circumstances shift significantly, they risk perpetuating this cycle of spending indefinitely, all while accruing interest rates as high as 22%.

It's imperative to understand that this pattern of behavior does not align with the principles of wealth accumulation. Relying on debt to finance unnecessary purchases is not a sound financial strategy, and it will not lead to true wealth. Instead, it's essential to adopt a more prudent approach to spending and debt management. By prioritizing investments that generate long-term returns and practicing disciplined financial habits, individuals can gradually build wealth and achieve financial security for themselves and their families.

Debt can indeed be a powerful tool when utilized effectively, yet many perceive it as inherently risky. However, it's crucial to recognize that it's not the debt itself that poses a risk, but rather the individuals managing it. When debt is managed responsibly and strategically, it can serve as a means to propel one towards financial prosperity and success.

For those who struggle to meet their financial obligations, such as credit card bills, car loans, or mortgages, the path to wealth can seem elusive. However, when debt is utilized judiciously and payments are made on time, it can be a catalyst for building assets and achieving long-term financial stability.

Contrary to common belief, many individuals leverage debt to create wealth and attain financial freedom. The key lies in understanding how to leverage debt effectively. By allocating a small portion of their funds to acquire a larger stake in an investment, individuals can multiply their returns exponentially. This concept, known as leverage, allows them to amplify their potential gains and accelerate their journey towards financial independence.

However, the benefits of leveraging debt extend beyond mere financial gain. When used strategically, debt can also provide individuals with access to valuable resources and opportunities that may otherwise be out of reach. By leveraging debt wisely, individuals can unlock doors to new ventures, expand their financial horizons, and ultimately achieve greater levels of success and fulfillment.

In essence, debt is not inherently good or bad—it's how we manage and utilize it that determines its impact on our financial well-being. By approaching debt with foresight, discipline, and a strategic mindset, individuals can harness its potential to build wealth, secure their financial future, and unlock a world of possibilities.

Let's go a little deeper into the concept of leveraging debt and its implications for asset ownership and wealth creation. When individuals utilize debt as a financial tool, they gain the ability to acquire assets without the need for full ownership. This strategic approach empowers borrowers to control valuable assets while minimizing their initial capital outlay.

The advantages of leveraging debt for asset acquisition are manifold. Firstly, it provides individuals with access to revenue streams generated by the asset, such as rental income from real estate properties or dividends from stocks. This additional income can serve as a valuable source of passive cash flow, supplementing one's regular earnings and contributing to overall financial stability. Leveraging debt allows individuals to benefit from the appreciation of the asset over time. As the value of the asset increases, so too does the borrower's equity stake in it, enabling them to build wealth and accumulate assets without significant upfront investment. This appreciation can result from various factors, including market demand, inflation, and improvements made to the asset itself.

Leveraging debt also provides individuals with tax advantages, including depreciation deductions. In many cases, borrowers can deduct depreciation expenses associated with the asset from their taxable income, reducing their overall tax liability and increasing their after-tax cash flow. This tax benefit serves as yet another incentive for leveraging debt as a means of asset acquisition.

Moreover, it allows individuals to enjoy the use and benefits of the asset without bearing the full financial burden of ownership. Whether it's a home, a business property, or a portfolio of investments, borrowers can leverage debt to gain access to assets that enhance their quality of life, support their financial goals, and contribute to their long-term prosperity.

In summary, leveraging debt to acquire assets offers numerous advantages, including access to revenue streams, potential appreciation, tax benefits, and the ability to enjoy the benefits of ownership without the need for full ownership. By strategically leveraging debt, individuals can enhance their financial flexibility, build wealth, and create a more secure and prosperous future for themselves and their families.

Long-term debt offers distinct advantages when it comes to managing financial obligations over extended periods. Opting for long-term debt entails spreading out the repayment of liabilities over several years, providing borrowers with several key benefits.

One of the primary advantages of long-term debt is that it allows individuals to make more manageable monthly payments. By stretching out the repayment schedule, borrowers can alleviate the financial strain associated with large lump-sum payments, making it easier to budget and plan for other expenses. This increased affordability offers individuals greater financial flexibility, enabling them to allocate funds towards savings, investments, or other priorities.it involves financing assets that have the potential to generate income or appreciate in value over time. For example, a mortgage on a home or a loan for a business property may be considered long-term debt. In such cases, the asset itself serves as collateral for the loan, meaning that as the asset appreciates or generates income, it can be used to pay off the debt.

long-term debt can be a strategic financial decision that not only makes monthly payments more manageable but also allows individuals to leverage assets to pay off liabilities over time. By carefully managing long-term debt and making timely payments, borrowers can achieve their financial goals while maintaining stability and security for the future.

Let's consider some big companies like Apple and Microsoft. 490 out of the Fortune 500 companies leverage debt to grow their fortunes. Wealthy individuals understand this strategy well.

Wealthy individuals often employ a sophisticated financial strategy known as asset leveraging. This strategy involves borrowing against assets that typically depreciate in value, such as real estate or machinery, to acquire assets that have the potential to appreciate over time, such as stocks, businesses, or investment properties.

By leveraging debt in this manner, wealthy individuals can maximize their returns on investment while minimizing their initial capital outlay. Rather than tying up large sums of their own money in appreciating assets, they use borrowed funds to finance the purchase, allowing them to maintain liquidity and preserve their cash reserves for other opportunities. By focusing on assets that offer potential for long-term growth and income generation, wealthy individuals can effectively leverage their borrowing power to build wealth and create passive income streams. This strategic approach to asset allocation enables them to diversify their investment portfolio, mitigate risk, and capitalize on market opportunities while maintaining control over their financial assets.

The key to successful asset leveraging lies in careful planning, risk management, and disciplined execution. Wealthy individuals understand the importance of maintaining a balance between debt and assets, ensuring that their borrowing activities align with their overall financial objectives and risk tolerance. By leveraging debt to acquire appreciating assets under controlled conditions, they can effectively grow their wealth and secure their financial future for generations to come.

Here are two controlled assets to consider when utilizing debt:

- Invest in yourself - Self-education, training, seminars, conferences, and mentorship are essential investments aimed at enhancing your competency in managing the asset class for which you plan to utilize debt. By continually developing your skills and knowledge, you increase your ability to make informed decisions and maximize the potential returns on your investments. Investing in yourself is a foundational step towards achieving financial success and independence.

- Invest in real estate - Real estate stands as the ultimate frontier for creating epic wealth through the strategic use of debt leveraging. By acquiring income-producing properties or properties with the potential for appreciation, investors can harness the power of leverage to multiply their returns and build substantial wealth over time. Real estate offers numerous advantages, including tax benefits, passive income streams, and the potential for long-term capital appreciation. With careful planning and due diligence, investing in real estate can be a lucrative strategy for achieving financial freedom and security.

For those who are uncertain about the concept of leveraging debt, I would like to illustrate the mathematics so you can relate it to your own resources, asset class, and financial goals.

Example: Let's say you purchase a house valued at $100,000. As a motivated seller, you acquire it at a discounted price of $80,000. You put down 20%, which is $16,000, and leverage the remaining 80% from the bank, totaling $64,000 in long-term debt.

Therefore, you have acquired $64,000 in debt, but without fully owning the property, you still maintain control over it. The tax advantages stemming from appreciation and amortization make the value of real estate a hedge against inflation, allowing you to use a small portion of your own money to leverage future acquisitions.

In the next step of the example, you find tenants who pay $1,200 monthly in rent. These rental payments go towards paying down the mortgage, contributing to amortization. Essentially, you are using debt to create income, and then using that income to pay off debt. Real estate offers tax advantages on debt payments and the cost of borrowing money, allowing you to potentially show a loss on paper while still realizing profits in the bank.

Appreciation isn't solely what defines real estate, and timing the market is not as crucial as one might assume. Assuming a conservative 3% appreciation rate, the value of the property appreciates to $110,000 per year after three years. Adding three years of debt pay-down, this results in principle equity at a 3% appreciation rate, totaling $36,000. Additionally, the principle pay-down amounts to $3,000, resulting in new equity of $49,000.

This is the concept I want you to understand: leveraging debt and how it's executed. Therefore, we've turned $16,000 into $49,000, a 300% increase in three years. With this newfound equity, you can leverage it into new debt and acquire more properties, repeating the process. In three years, you can repeat this process, acquiring properties and potentially acquiring 13 properties in less than 10 years through leveraging.

What happens when a person is overleveraged? It means they have borrowed too much money and are unable to make interest payments, principle payments, and operating expenses. Managing debt becomes a struggle, and their financial situation prevents them from covering expenses. In such cases, banks may step in and take possession of the property, often selling it at a discount.

Interestingly, the more debt you have, the more money you can make. This increased income then allows you to acquire even more debt. This is precisely how wealthy individuals leverage debt to build their wealth. While the process may appear slow initially, it gains momentum and snowballs when executed correctly.

To summarize:

> We understand what debt is,
>
> Why we should use debt to become wealthy,
>
> Where to leverage debt,
>
> How it works once you begin,
>
> And when to use debt.

Money is borrowed against a depreciating asset to acquire income-producing assets. The more you use debt, the faster wealth can be created, leading to financial independence.

Contrary to common belief, debt is not inherently risky. In fact, many people, such as contractors, property managers—who are responsible for managing properties, finding tenants, and handling repairs—and investors, utilize debt as a tool to build wealth. Without leveraging debt, your chances of creating wealth are limited, and you may struggle throughout your life.

Investing in real estate is a process, and mistakes will inevitably occur—I certainly made them with my first property. However, with practice, you gain confidence. Consider how you can increase cash flow by purchasing properties. For instance, if you earn $700 per year from rent on one property, purchasing another property that generates the same amount doubles your cash flow from real estate.

The first deal may be challenging, but don't be afraid to take a chance—you have to start somewhere. Investing in real estate creates a stream of cash flow that can lead to long-term financial stability and success.

Let's examine an example to better illustrate this point:

Example:

A property is purchased for $100,000, offering a 7% cash return on your investment, which equates to $7,000 annually. This cash flow protects against the absence of debt.

There are various methods to finance deals. For instance, the $100,000 purchase could be funded through finding investors or utilizing creative financing options.

Most people looking to invest in real estate can do so with significant cash savings, which enables them to invest in properties over the long term. This approach has undoubtedly proven to be effective. However, we strongly advise conducting thorough due diligence on a property before making any investment decisions. Real estate is a great way to safeguard money, as it offers tax benefits and the potential to generate cash flow.

Now, let's consider an example: the value of the property can be depreciated over 27.5 years, allowing you to deduct from your annual income profits. It's important to note that building always depreciates, not land.

Here are three ways wealthy people invest in real estate:

- Tax Breaks: These are deductions provided by the government, also known as tax write-offs. It's advisable to consult with a tax accountant to receive guidance and advice on transactions, ensuring you maximize your tax benefits while staying compliant with tax laws.

- Depreciation: Properties experience wear and tear over time, leading to depreciation in their value. Investors can benefit from write-offs in taxes by leveraging this depreciation, even considering the overall value of the property. It's a valuable strategy to reduce taxable income and increase cash flow.

- Underperforming Residential Properties: Investors can generate yield from rental income by investing in properties that are currently underperforming. With strategic renovations or management improvements, these properties can be transformed into lucrative income-producing assets.

Creating wealth through real estate is a long-term endeavor. It's essential to invest in income-producing assets that can generate cash flow and appreciation over time. By doing so, you not only secure your financial future but also create a legacy that can benefit future generations.

NOTES:

CHAPTER 12

JENNIFER NICOLE LEE

MINDFUL LIVING: STRESS MANAGEMENT TECHNIQUES FOR PEAK PERFORMANCE

In today's fast-paced world, stress has become a common companion for many individuals striving for success. The demands of modern life, whether they stem from work, family, or personal goals, can often feel overwhelming, leaving us feeling drained and depleted. However, amidst the chaos and challenges, there lies an opportunity to cultivate resilience and thrive through the practice of mindful living.

Mastering the art of mindful living is not merely about managing stress; it's about transforming our relationship with it. It's about learning to navigate the ups and downs of life with grace and presence, rather than allowing stress to dictate our experiences. By incorporating mindfulness into our daily lives, we can tap into a reservoir of inner strength and wisdom that enables us to face adversity with clarity and composure.

In this chapter, we provide insight into various stress management techniques that can empower you to achieve peak performance in both your financial and physical fitness pursuits. From yoga and meditation to breathing exercises and positive mindset practices, each technique offers a unique pathway to cultivating resilience and well-being.

By exploring these techniques and integrating them into your daily routine, you'll not only enhance your ability to manage stress but also unlock your full potential in every aspect of your life. Whether you're striving for financial success, pursuing physical fitness goals, or simply seeking greater balance and fulfillment, the principles of mindful living can guide you on your journey towards greater happiness and success. So, let's embark on this transformative journey together, and discover the power of mindful living to create a life of purpose, passion, and peace.

Yoga, originating from ancient India, has evolved into a diverse and multifaceted practice that encompasses various styles and approaches. Each style of yoga offers unique benefits, catering to different preferences, fitness levels, and goals. Let's explore some of the most popular styles of yoga and their specific benefits:

Hatha Yoga:

- Benefits: Hatha yoga focuses on the fundamental principles of yoga, emphasizing physical postures (asanas) and breath control (pranayama). It is suitable for beginners and helps improve flexibility, strength, and balance. Hatha yoga also promotes relaxation and stress reduction through mindful movement and breath awareness.

Vinyasa Yoga:

- Benefits: Vinyasa yoga, often referred to as "flow" yoga, synchronizes breath with movement, creating a dynamic and fluid practice. It builds cardiovascular endurance, enhances flexibility, and strengthens muscles. Vinyasa yoga also fosters mindfulness and mental focus as practitioners move through sequences of poses with intention and awareness.

Ashtanga Yoga:

- Benefits: Ashtanga yoga follows a specific sequence of postures linked together by breath, providing a structured and disciplined practice. It builds strength, endurance, and stamina while promoting detoxification and purification of the body. Ashtanga yoga also cultivates mental resilience and concentration through repetitive movement and breath control.

Bikram Yoga:

- Benefits: Bikram yoga, also known as "hot" yoga, consists of a series of 26 postures practiced in a heated room. The heat increases flexibility, facilitates detoxification, and improves circulation. Bikram yoga also promotes mental focus and stress reduction as practitioners challenge themselves in a challenging environment.

Yin Yoga:

- Benefits: Yin yoga involves holding passive poses for an extended period, targeting the deep connective tissues and fascia in the body. It improves flexibility, releases tension, and enhances joint mobility. Yin yoga also promotes relaxation and mindfulness, allowing practitioners to surrender to the present moment and cultivate inner stillness.

Restorative Yoga:

- Benefits: Restorative yoga focuses on relaxation and rejuvenation, using props such as blankets, bolsters, and blocks to support the body in gentle, passive poses. It reduces stress, promotes deep relaxation, and restores balance to the nervous system. Restorative yoga is especially beneficial for relieving tension and fatigue, making it ideal for those recovering from injury or illness.

Kundalini Yoga:

- Benefits: Kundalini yoga combines dynamic movement, breathwork, chanting, and meditation to awaken spiritual energy and promote self-awareness. It strengthens the nervous system, balances the glandular system, and enhances mental clarity and intuition. Kundalini yoga also fosters emotional healing and resilience, helping practitioners access their inner wisdom and vitality.

By exploring different styles of yoga and finding the one that resonates with you, you can harness the transformative power of this ancient practice to improve your physical health, mental well-being, and overall quality of life. Whether you prefer a vigorous flow or a gentle restorative practice, yoga offers a holistic approach to wellness that nourishes the body, mind, and spirit.

Breathing exercises are a cornerstone of mindfulness practices, offering immediate relief from stress and anxiety while promoting a sense of calm and well-being. Here are some popular breathing techniques, each with its unique benefits:

Deep Belly Breathing (Diaphragmatic Breathing):

- Benefits: Deep belly breathing engages the diaphragm, allowing you to take slow, deep breaths that fully expand the lungs. This technique promotes relaxation, reduces stress, and lowers blood pressure. It also improves oxygen flow to the brain, enhancing mental clarity and focus.

Alternate Nostril Breathing (Nadi Shodhana):

- Benefits: Alternate nostril breathing balances the flow of energy in the body, harmonizing the left and right hemispheres of the brain. It calms the mind, relieves tension, and enhances concentration and awareness. Alternate nostril breathing also purifies the nadis (energy channels) and promotes overall well-being.

Box Breathing (Square Breathing):

- Benefits: Box breathing involves inhaling, holding, exhaling, and holding the breath in equal counts, creating a square-shaped breath pattern. This technique regulates the nervous system, inducing a state of calm and relaxation. Box breathing also improves oxygenation, reduces stress hormones, and enhances mental resilience and focus.

4-7-8 Breathing (Relaxing Breath):

- Benefits: The 4-7-8 breathing technique involves inhaling for four counts, holding the breath for seven counts, and exhaling for eight counts. This pattern triggers the body's relaxation response, promoting deep relaxation and stress relief. 4-7-8 breathing also helps alleviate insomnia, anxiety, and panic attacks.

Ujjayi Breathing (Victorious Breath):

- Benefits: Ujjayi breathing involves constricting the back of the throat to create a soft, audible whispering sound during inhalation and exhalation. This technique calms the nervous system, regulates the breath, and generates internal heat. Ujjayi breathing also enhances focus, endurance, and mindfulness during yoga and meditation practices.

Kapalabhati Breathing (Skull-Shining Breath):

- Benefits: Kapalabhati breathing involves rapid, forceful exhalations followed by passive inhalations, creating a pumping motion in the abdomen. This technique increases oxygenation, energizes the body, and clears the mind of stagnant energy and toxins. Kapalabhati breathing also stimulates digestion, improves circulation, and enhances mental clarity.

Sama Vritti (Equal Breathing):

- Benefits: Sama vritti involves inhaling and exhaling for an equal count, creating a balanced and rhythmic breath pattern. This technique calms the nervous system, promotes relaxation, and balances the mind. Sama vritti breathing also enhances concentration, awareness, and emotional stability.

Incorporating these breathing exercises into your daily routine can provide immediate relief from stress and tension while fostering a deeper connection to your body and breath. Experiment with different techniques to find the ones that resonate with you, and practice regularly to cultivate a greater sense of calm, balance, and well-being in your life.

Movement is not only crucial for maintaining physical health but also plays a significant role in managing stress and enhancing mental well-being. Here's why incorporating regular physical activity into your routine is essential for stress management:

- Stress Reduction: Physical activity triggers the release of endorphins, neurotransmitters in the brain that act as natural mood lifters. Exercise helps reduce levels of stress hormones like cortisol and adrenaline, leading to a decrease in feelings of tension and anxiety. Engaging in movement can provide a much-needed break from the pressures of daily life, allowing you to clear your mind and focus on the present moment.

- Mood Enhancement: Movement stimulates the production of serotonin and dopamine, neurotransmitters associated with feelings of happiness and well-being. Regular physical activity has been shown to alleviate symptoms of depression and improve overall mood. Whether it's a brisk walk in nature or a high-energy dance class, finding activities that you enjoy can uplift your spirits and boost your mental outlook.

- Energy Boost: While it may seem counterintuitive, expending energy through movement can actually increase your overall energy levels. Regular exercise improves circulation, delivers oxygen and nutrients to your cells more efficiently, and enhances cardiovascular health. As a result, you'll likely experience increased vitality and endurance, allowing you to tackle daily challenges with greater resilience and vigor.

- Stress Release: Movement provides a healthy outlet for releasing pent-up stress and tension from the body. Physical activity encourages deep breathing, muscle relaxation, and the discharge of nervous energy, helping to alleviate physical symptoms of stress such as muscle tightness and headaches. Engaging in activities like yoga, tai chi, or Pilates can promote relaxation and restore balance to both body and mind.

- Cognitive Benefits: Exercise has been shown to enhance cognitive function and mental clarity. Physical activity increases blood flow to the brain, which can improve focus, concentration, and memory. Regular movement also stimulates the growth of new brain cells and neural connections, which may help protect against cognitive decline and age-related memory loss.

Incorporating movement into your daily routine doesn't have to involve intense workouts or lengthy gym sessions.

Simple activities like gardening, playing with your pets, or taking the stairs instead of the elevator can all contribute to your overall physical activity level. The key is to find activities that you enjoy and that fit seamlessly into your lifestyle, making movement a natural and enjoyable part of your day. By prioritizing regular physical activity, you can reap the numerous benefits for your physical, mental, and emotional well-being, ultimately leading to a happier, healthier life.

Self-care is not selfish; it's essential for maintaining your overall well-being and managing stress effectively. Here's why prioritizing self-care activities is crucial for promoting mental, emotional, and physical health:

- Stress Reduction: Engaging in self-care activities allows you to step away from the pressures and responsibilities of daily life, giving your mind and body a chance to unwind and relax. Whether it's taking a warm bath, practicing mindfulness meditation, or enjoying a leisurely walk in nature, self-care activities help to reduce cortisol levels and promote a sense of calm and tranquility.
- Improved Mood: Investing time in activities that bring you joy and pleasure can have a significant impact on your mood and emotional well-being. Whether it's indulging in a favorite hobby, spending time with loved ones, or treating yourself to a spa day, self-care activities stimulate the release of feel-good neurotransmitters like serotonin and

dopamine, leading to improved mood and overall happiness.

- Enhanced Resilience: Prioritizing self-care fosters resilience and helps build emotional strength and coping skills. Taking time to care for yourself allows you to recharge your batteries and build up your reserves, making you better equipped to handle life's challenges and setbacks when they arise. Self-care activities provide a buffer against stress and burnout, allowing you to bounce back more quickly and effectively.

- Increased Productivity: Contrary to popular belief, self-care is not a waste of time; it's an investment in your overall productivity and effectiveness. When you prioritize self-care, you're better able to focus, concentrate, and perform at your best in all areas of your life. Taking regular breaks and engaging in activities that rejuvenate and refresh you can actually boost your productivity and creativity over the long term.

- Better Relationships: When you prioritize self-care, you're better able to show up as your best self in your relationships with others. By taking care of your own needs and nurturing your own well-being, you have more to give to those around you. When you're feeling refreshed, rejuvenated, and emotionally balanced, you're better able to connect with others and foster healthy, fulfilling relationships.

Types of Self-Care Activities:

- Spa Day: Treat yourself to a day of pampering at a spa, where you can enjoy massages, facials, and other relaxing treatments designed to soothe your body and mind.

- Nature Walk: Spend time outdoors in nature, whether it's going for a hike in the mountains, walking along the beach, or simply sitting in a park and soaking up the sights and sounds of the natural world.

- Creative Expression: Engage in creative activities that bring you joy and allow you to express yourself, such as painting, writing, dancing, or playing music.

- Mindfulness Meditation: Practice mindfulness meditation to cultivate present-moment awareness and reduce stress. Focus on your breath, body sensations, or the sounds around you to bring your attention into the here and now.

- Social Connection: Spend quality time with friends and loved ones, whether it's having a meaningful conversation, sharing a meal together, or engaging in a fun activity that you both enjoy.

- Digital Detox: Take a break from screens and technology to give your mind a rest and reconnect with the world around you. Unplug from devices and spend time engaging in offline activities that nourish your soul.

- Restorative Sleep: Prioritize getting enough sleep each night to allow your body and mind to rest and rejuvenate. Create a calming bedtime routine and create a comfortable sleep environment to promote restorative sleep.

By incorporating self-care activities into your daily routine, you can cultivate a greater sense of well-being, reduce stress levels, and enhance your overall quality of life. Remember that self-care is not a luxury; it's a necessity for living a happy, healthy, and balanced life.

Cultivating a positive mindset is not just about seeing the glass as half full; it's about developing a mental attitude that empowers you to navigate life's challenges with resilience, optimism, and grace. Here are some strategies for cultivating a positive mindset and managing stress effectively:

- Practice Gratitude: Take time each day to reflect on the things you're grateful for, whether it's your health, relationships, or simple pleasures like a beautiful sunrise or a delicious meal. Cultivating an attitude of gratitude can help shift your focus away from what's lacking or negative in your life and towards the abundance and blessings that surround you.

- Focus on the Present Moment: Instead of dwelling on the past or worrying about the future, practice mindfulness and focus on the present moment. Mindfulness techniques such as deep breathing, body scanning, and sensory awareness can help anchor you in the here and now, reducing stress and promoting inner peace.

- Reframe Negative Thoughts: When faced with negative thoughts or challenges, practice reframing them into positive affirmations or empowering beliefs. For example, instead of thinking, "I'll never be able to do this," reframe it as, "I am capable and resourceful, and I can overcome any obstacle that comes my way." By consciously choosing to focus on positive thoughts and beliefs, you can rewire your brain for optimism and resilience.

- Surround Yourself with Positivity: Pay attention to the people you surround yourself with and the media you consume. Surround yourself with positive, supportive individuals who uplift and inspire you, and limit exposure to negative influences such as news stories or social media content that triggers stress or anxiety.

- Practice Self-Compassion: Treat yourself with kindness, compassion, and understanding, especially during times of difficulty or failure. Instead of berating yourself for mistakes or shortcomings, practice self-compassion and remind yourself that you're only human and deserving of love and forgiveness.

- Set Realistic Goals: Set yourself up for success by setting realistic, achievable goals that align with your values and priorities. Break larger goals down into smaller, actionable steps, and celebrate your progress along the way. By setting yourself up for success, you'll boost your confidence and motivation to continue moving forward.

- Cultivate Positive Relationships: Surround yourself with supportive, positive people who uplift and inspire you. Cultivate meaningful relationships with friends, family, and mentors who share your values and encourage you to be the best version of yourself.

- Practice Resilience: Life is full of ups and downs, and setbacks are inevitable. Instead of viewing challenges as insurmountable obstacles, practice resilience and see them as opportunities for growth and learning. Embrace failure as a natural part of the journey and use setbacks as stepping stones to success.

By incorporating these strategies into your daily life, you can cultivate a positive mindset that empowers you to manage stress effectively, overcome challenges, and live with greater joy, purpose, and fulfillment. Remember that positivity is a choice, and with practice, you can train your mind to see the good in every situation and embrace life with optimism and enthusiasm.

Visualization is a powerful tool that harnesses the mind's ability to create vivid mental images of desired outcomes. When you engage in visualization techniques, you're essentially programming your subconscious mind to align with your conscious goals and aspirations. Here's how you can expand on the concept of visualization and its benefits:

- Clarify Your Goals: Before you begin visualizing, it's essential to have clarity about what you want to achieve. Take some time to define your goals with specificity, whether they're related to fitness, career, relationships, or personal development. The clearer your goals, the more effective your visualization practice will be.

- Create a Detailed Mental Image: Close your eyes and imagine yourself accomplishing your goals in vivid detail. Picture yourself in the exact scenario you desire, whether it's crossing the finish line of a race, delivering a successful presentation, or achieving financial abundance. Engage all your senses to make the visualization as lifelike as possible, imagining the sights, sounds, smells, and feelings associated with success.

- Harness Emotions: Visualization becomes even more potent when you infuse it with positive emotions. As you visualize yourself achieving your goals, tap into the feelings of joy, excitement, pride, and fulfillment that accompany success. Embody the emotions as if you've already accomplished your goals, allowing yourself to experience the pleasure and satisfaction of achievement.

- Repetition and Consistency: Like any skill, visualization improves with practice and repetition. Set aside time each day to engage in visualization exercises, preferably in a quiet, distraction-free environment where you can fully immerse yourself in the practice. Consistency is key to reprogramming your subconscious mind and reinforcing positive mental patterns.

- Overcome Limiting Beliefs: Visualization can also be used to overcome limiting beliefs and self-doubt that may be holding you back from achieving your goals. As you visualize success, challenge and reframe any negative thoughts or beliefs that arise. Replace them with empowering affirmations and images of yourself succeeding against all odds.

- Use Visualization as a Preparation Tool: Visualization isn't just about mental rehearsal; it can also be a powerful preparation tool for upcoming challenges or events. Athletes, performers, and public speakers often use visualization to mentally rehearse their performances, enhancing their confidence and readiness to excel when the time comes.

- Review and Reflect: After each visualization session, take a moment to reflect on your experience. Notice any shifts in your mindset, mood, or perception of your goals. Pay attention to any insights or intuitive guidance that may arise during the practice. Regular reflection can deepen your understanding of yourself and your goals, leading to greater clarity and motivation.

By incorporating visualization into your daily routine, you can harness the power of your mind to manifest your deepest desires and create the life you envision. Whether you're striving for personal, professional, or athletic success, visualization can be a valuable tool for unlocking your full potential and achieving your dreams.

Meditation is a transformative practice that cultivates mindfulness, presence, and inner tranquility. It involves intentionally directing your attention inward, quieting the chatter of the mind, and connecting with the present moment. Here's how you can expand on the concept of meditation and its profound benefits:

- Mindfulness Meditation: One of the most popular forms of meditation, mindfulness meditation involves paying attention to the present moment with openness and curiosity. Sit comfortably, close your eyes, and focus on your breath, sensations in your body, or sounds in your environment. When thoughts or distractions arise, gently bring your attention back to the present moment without judgment.

- Guided Meditation: Guided meditation involves following the voice of a teacher or guide who leads you through a series of relaxation and visualization exercises. Guided meditations can be especially helpful for beginners or those seeking specific outcomes, such as stress reduction, self-love, or inner healing. You can find guided meditation recordings online or through meditation apps.

- Body Scan Meditation: Body scan meditation involves systematically scanning your body from head to toe, paying attention to any sensations or areas of tension. Start at the top of your head and gradually move down to your feet, bringing awareness to each part of your body with gentle curiosity and acceptance. Body scan meditation can help release physical tension and promote relaxation.

- Loving-kindness Meditation: Also known as metta meditation, loving-kindness meditation involves cultivating feelings of love, compassion, and goodwill towards yourself and others. Begin by directing loving-kindness towards yourself, then gradually extend it to loved ones, acquaintances, and even those with whom you may have difficulty. This practice can foster greater empathy, connection, and emotional resilience.

- Breath Awareness Meditation: Breath awareness meditation focuses on observing the natural rhythm of your breath without trying to control it. Sit quietly and bring your attention to the sensation of your breath as it enters and leaves your body. Notice the rise and fall of your chest or the sensation of air passing through your nostrils. Breath awareness meditation can help calm the mind, reduce anxiety, and increase present-moment awareness.

- Mantra Meditation: Mantra meditation involves repeating a sacred word, phrase, or sound silently or aloud to focus the mind and induce a state of deep concentration. Choose a mantra that resonates with you, such as "peace," "love," or "I am." Repeat the mantra with each inhale and exhale, allowing it to anchor your attention and quiet the mental chatter. Mantra meditation can promote relaxation, clarity, and spiritual connection.

- Walking Meditation: For those who struggle with sitting meditation, walking meditation offers an alternative way to cultivate mindfulness and presence. Take a slow, deliberate walk in a quiet, natural setting, focusing on the sensations of each step, the movement of your body, and the sights and sounds around you. Walking meditation can be a refreshing way to clear the mind, reduce stress, and reconnect with the beauty of the present moment.

- Consistency and Patience: Like any skill, meditation requires consistent practice and patience to experience its full benefits. Start with just a few minutes of meditation each day and gradually increase the duration as you become more comfortable with the practice. Remember that meditation is not about achieving a particular state or outcome but rather about cultivating awareness and acceptance of whatever arises in the present moment.

By incorporating meditation into your daily routine, you can cultivate a greater sense of calm, clarity, and inner peace amidst the challenges of life. Whether you're seeking stress relief, emotional balance, or spiritual growth, meditation can be a powerful tool for nurturing your well-being and awakening to the fullness of life.

Laughter is indeed a powerful antidote to stress, tension, and negativity, offering a natural and enjoyable way to uplift your spirits and enhance your overall well-being. Here's how you can expand on the importance of laughter and incorporate it into your stress management routine:

- Physical Benefits of Laughter: When you laugh, your body releases endorphins, often referred to as "feel-good" hormones, which can help alleviate pain, reduce stress, and boost your mood. Laughter also triggers the release of dopamine, a neurotransmitter associated with pleasure and reward, promoting a sense of relaxation and happiness.

- Stress Reduction: Laughter serves as a natural stress reliever, helping to decrease levels of cortisol, the body's primary stress hormone. By engaging in laughter regularly, you can lower your overall stress levels, improve resilience to stressors, and create a more positive outlook on life.

- Improvement in Mood: Laughter has a profound effect on your emotional state, lifting your spirits and fostering a sense of joy and connection with others. Whether you're sharing a joke with friends, watching a comedy show, or reminiscing about funny memories, laughter can instantly brighten your mood and create a sense of camaraderie.

- Enhanced Immune Function: Studies have shown that laughter can strengthen the immune system by increasing the production of immune cells and antibodies, which help defend the body against infections and illnesses. By incorporating laughter into your daily routine, you can bolster your immune function and promote overall health and vitality.

- Social Connection: Laughter is often a social activity, bringing people together and strengthening bonds between friends, family members, and colleagues. Shared laughter fosters a sense of connection, trust, and intimacy, creating positive relationships and enhancing social support networks.

- Laughter Yoga: Laughter yoga is a unique form of exercise that combines laughter exercises with deep breathing techniques derived from yoga. In laughter yoga sessions, participants engage in playful activities and laughter exercises designed to induce genuine laughter and promote relaxation. Laughter yoga can be practiced alone or in groups and is an effective way to reduce stress, boost mood, and improve overall well-being.

- Daily Practice: Make laughter a regular part of your daily routine by seeking out opportunities for humor and lightheartedness. Watch a comedy show or movie, listen to funny podcasts or stand-up comedy routines, or spend time with friends who have a good sense of humor. Even incorporating playful activities into your day, such as playing with pets or engaging in silly games, can elicit laughter and uplift your spirits.

- Laughter Meditation: Incorporate laughter into your meditation practice by engaging in laughter meditation techniques. Start by sitting comfortably and taking a few deep breaths to center yourself. Then, imagine yourself surrounded by joy and laughter, allowing yourself to laugh freely and spontaneously. As you continue to visualize laughter, notice how it uplifts your mood and creates a sense of lightness and positivity within you.

By embracing the power of laughter and incorporating it into your daily life, you can effectively manage stress, improve your mood, and enhance your overall quality of life. Whether you're sharing a hearty laugh with friends or indulging in a good comedy, remember that laughter truly is the best medicine for a happy and healthy life.

- Relaxing Music: Music has the power to soothe the soul and calm the mind. Create a playlist of your favorite relaxing tunes to listen to during moments of stress or tension, allowing the music to transport you to a state of tranquility and peace.

- Stretching: Incorporating stretching exercises into your routine can help release physical tension and promote relaxation. Take breaks throughout the day to stretch your muscles, focusing on areas that feel tight or tense.

- Positive Mindset Coach: Having a positive mindset coach or mentor to support you on your journey can be invaluable for managing stress and staying focused on your goals. A coach can provide guidance, encouragement, and perspective during challenging times, helping you see the light in dark moments and stay on track towards success.

In conclusion, mastering the art of mindful living is essential for managing stress effectively and achieving peak performance in all areas of your life. By incorporating yoga, breathing exercises, movement, self-care, positive mindset practices, visualization, meditation, laughter, relaxing music, stretching, and seeking support from a positive mindset coach, you can cultivate resilience, inner peace, and success on your journey towards financial and physical fitness. Remember, the power to thrive lies within you – embrace the journey and live mindfully each day.

NOTES:

CHAPTER 13

ALKA SHARMA

RETIREMENT PLANNING: SECURING YOUR FINANCIAL FUTURE

Retirement planning is not just about setting aside funds for your post-working years; it's a comprehensive strategy designed to ensure financial security and stability throughout your retirement. One of the primary objectives of retirement planning is to prevent the scenario of running out of money during retirement—a concern that many individuals face as they approach their golden years.

By engaging in retirement planning, individuals can assess their current financial situation, set realistic retirement goals, and develop a roadmap to achieve those goals. This involves evaluating sources of income, such as pensions, Social Security benefits, and personal savings, as well as estimating future expenses, including healthcare costs, living expenses, and leisure activities.

Through careful planning and prudent financial management, individuals can create a retirement savings portfolio that is diversified, resilient, and capable of generating sustainable income throughout retirement. This may involve investing in a mix of assets, such as stocks, bonds, real estate, and annuities, to balance risk and return and maximize long-term growth potential.

planning allows individuals to anticipate potential financial challenges and proactively implement strategies to mitigate risks. This could include factors such as inflation, market volatility, unexpected expenses, and longevity risk—the risk of outliving one's retirement savings. By incorporating contingencies and safety nets into their retirement plan, individuals can safeguard against unforeseen circumstances and ensure financial resilience in retirement.

It's about achieving peace of mind and financial freedom in your later years. By taking proactive steps to plan for retirement, individuals can enjoy a fulfilling and worry-free retirement, knowing that they have the financial resources to support their lifestyle and achieve their dreams well into the future.

Planning for retirement is a crucial step in managing how money is spent, saved, and managed. By creating a secure financial plan, you can map out your goals and gain confidence in your day-to-day finances. This not only provides a sense of purpose and joy but also offers peace of mind, knowing that you are prepared for the future. A well-thought-out retirement plan allows you to align your financial resources with your lifestyle aspirations, ensuring that you can enjoy the retirement you've always dreamed of.

It also empowers you to make informed decisions about investments, expenses, and savings strategies, maximizing your financial security and independence in your later years. Ultimately, planning for retirement sets the stage for a fulfilling and rewarding chapter of life, where you can pursue your passions, explore new opportunities, and enjoy the fruits of your labor with confidence and peace of mind.

Retirement is often defined as the period in one's life when they cease regular employment and transition into a phase of leisure, relaxation, and potentially pursuing personal interests or hobbies. For many individuals, the traditional retirement age is around 65 years old, at which point they hope to have accumulated sufficient savings in retirement accounts to support themselves financially without the need for employment.

Having a 401(k), Social Security benefits, or RRSP (Registered Retirement Savings Plan in Canada) can provide a solid financial foundation for enjoying your golden years to the fullest. These retirement savings vehicles offer a source of income that can help cover essential expenses, such as housing, healthcare, and daily living costs, allowing retirees to maintain a comfortable standard of living.

Accounts can also provide a cushion for unexpected expenses or emergencies that may arise during retirement. Whether it's covering medical bills, home repairs, or travel expenses, having a reliable source of income from retirement savings can alleviate financial stress and provide peace of mind.

Retirement benefits can enable retirees to pursue their passions and interests without the constraints of financial worries. Whether it's traveling the world, pursuing hobbies, or spending quality time with family and friends, having financial security in retirement allows individuals to embrace new experiences and make the most of their leisure time.

s and can serve as a legacy for future generations, providing a financial safety net for loved ones and ensuring a lasting impact beyond one's lifetime. By responsibly managing and maximizing the benefits of 401(k), Social Security, or RRSP accounts, individuals can create a foundation for a fulfilling and enjoyable retirement that reflects their values, aspirations, and dreams.

Retirement is undeniably one of life's most significant and final decisions. Allow me to share a quote that resonates deeply in this context:

> "There's no one-size-fits-all solution for retirement income; what works best for you depends on your individual goals and comfort levels."

This quote succinctly highlights the diversity of approaches to retirement planning and emphasizes the importance of tailoring your strategy to align with your unique financial objectives and risk tolerance. While the journey towards retirement may present varying levels of risk, investments remain a fundamental avenue for securing retirement income.

Among the plethora of retirement strategies, the 4% rule has emerged as a standard approach. Though not infallible, this guideline suggests that retirees can safely withdraw 4% of their retirement savings annually, adjusting for inflation. Studies have shown that adhering to this rule provides retirees with a 95% chance of not outliving their savings—an essential reassurance in retirement planning.

For retirees embarking on their investment journey, a key consideration is asset allocation. Experts recommend allocating between 50% to 75% of retirement investments to stocks, balancing potential growth opportunities with risk management. This balanced approach helps retirees maintain a diversified portfolio, mitigating the impact of market volatility while striving for long-term financial stability and growth.

To ensure financial security well into your 80s and 90s, a well-crafted plan is essential. This plan should include asset allocation, which involves finding the right balance of stocks and bonds to sustain your desired lifestyle even in the face of economic downturns, inflation, fluctuations in interest rates, and potential health challenges.

What would be an ideal asset allocation?

The best approach hinges on your investment strategies and the need to withdraw income as required. The most significant risk retirees face is known as sequence of returns risk.

Allow me to illustrate with an example: Suppose a retiree has a $1 million nest egg, retired in 2022, invested in S&P 500 companies, and withdraws $4,000 per month to maintain their desired lifestyle.

The risk arises when withdrawals are made from underperforming investments at the start of retirement, increasing the likelihood of running out of money rapidly. As the stock market's sequence of events is unpredictable, it's crucial to segment your funds based on income needs during different time frames to safeguard your desired lifestyle and build wealth while protecting short-term income needs.

This concept of segmenting investable assets is commonly referred to as 'bucketing.' Here's the framework:

- Money needed for immediate retirement goals should be allocated to assets that do not lose principal, such as high-yield savings accounts, cash, or treasuries.
- Money needed for the next 5-15 years of retirement should be invested in a balanced portfolio, comprising a mix of treasury bonds, dividend

stocks, and index funds. This allocation provides both income and steady growth.

- The third bucket contains funds that will not be touched for at least 15 years. Here, a long-term strategy is adopted, with investments in stocks, REITs (Real Estate Investment Trusts), metals like gold and silver. This strategy offers the highest growth potential over the long term.

As you age, it's important to gradually transition to selling these stocks while maintaining your desired lifestyle. It's recommended to review and potentially trim your stocks every 10 years to capitalize on their highest growth potential before selling off a portion of your investment.

However, in our ever-evolving economic environment, marked by high-interest rates and stock market volatility, the application of the 4% rule may vary. Sequence risk is primarily triggered by cash flow fluctuations, emphasizing the importance of careful financial planning and asset allocation.

Most people are unprepared for retirement. Statistics from the Federal Reserve show that 41% of individuals over the age of 60 do not have savings on track. This highlights the importance of understanding how much you can comfortably spend in retirement, regardless of market fluctuations and inflation, to ensure your money will not run out.

Approaching retirement, it's crucial to assess what retirement looks like for you. Consider questions such as when you want to retire and how much you plan to spend. Start by itemizing your current spending and projecting how it may change in retirement. This list should include expenses such as utilities, property taxes, entertainment, food, and insurance. Additionally, factor in annual healthcare costs if you plan to retire before the age of 65. Other considerations, like purchasing a new car every five years, should also be accounted for.

As you age, your spending priorities may shift. For example, travel expenses may decrease as you reach older age brackets. Determine your ideal budget for vacation and travel expenses accordingly. Additionally, consider any funding you may want to allocate towards grandchildren's college education. Decide how much you aim to contribute annually and calculate how this will impact your retirement savings.

Consulting with a financial advisor can help you allocate funds towards various goals, such as contributing to your children's college savings plans. The goal of these discussions is to identify what is important for you in retirement—whether it's retiring sooner, giving generously to charities, embarking on new adventures, or spending more freely than you might have anticipated. By carefully planning and considering your financial priorities, you can create a retirement strategy that aligns with your goals and aspirations.

NOTES:

CHAPTER 14

JENNIFER NICOLE LEE

REST AND RECOVERY: THE IMPORTANCE OF RECOVERY FOR LONGTERM FITNESS SUCCESS

"Recovery is the New Workout"
-Jennifer Nicole Lee

In the pursuit of physical fitness, our society tends to glorify intense workouts and relentless dedication to pushing our bodies to the limit. We're bombarded with images of athletes pushing themselves to new extremes, often leading us to believe that more is always better. However, what many fail to realize is that true fitness success isn't solely determined by how hard we push ourselves during workouts. It's also about recognizing the importance of allowing our bodies the necessary time to rest and recover.

In this fast-paced world, we're conditioned to believe that constantly pushing ourselves harder is the only path to success. We're encouraged to hit the gym harder, run faster, lift heavier weights, and do more reps. While pushing ourselves outside our comfort zones is essential for growth, it's equally important to recognize that our bodies need time to repair and rebuild in between these intense sessions. Without adequate rest and recovery, we risk burnout, overtraining, and injury, ultimately hindering our long-term fitness progress.

In this chapter, we'll delve deep into the critical role that rest and recovery play in achieving lasting fitness success. We'll explore the physiological processes that occur during rest periods, the benefits of prioritizing recovery strategies, and practical tips for incorporating restorative practices into your fitness routine. By understanding the symbiotic relationship between intense workouts and proper recovery, you'll be empowered to optimize your training regimen and unlock your full potential. Remember, in the journey to fitness excellence, "Recovery is the New Workout," and it's time to give it the attention and respect it deserves.

Rest is the unsung hero of the fitness journey, often overlooked in favor of more intense workouts and rigorous training schedules. However, its importance cannot be overstated when it comes to optimizing physical performance and overall well-being. Adequate rest periods between workouts are not merely a luxury but a necessity for the body to recover and adapt to the stresses imposed upon it during exercise.

When we engage in strenuous physical activity, we place a significant amount of stress on our muscles, joints, and nervous system. This stress is essential for triggering adaptations that lead to improvements in strength, endurance, and cardiovascular fitness. However, without sufficient rest, the body is unable to repair the damage caused by exercise and adapt effectively to the training stimulus.

Rest periods allow the body to replenish depleted energy stores, repair damaged muscle fibers, and remove metabolic waste products accumulated during exercise. This process, known as muscle protein synthesis, is crucial for muscle growth and repair. Without adequate rest, the body becomes susceptible to overtraining, a condition characterized by persistent fatigue, decreased performance, and increased risk of injury.

In addition to physical recovery, rest also plays a vital role in mental and emotional well-being. Intense exercise can take a toll on the nervous system, leading to feelings of fatigue, irritability, and decreased motivation. Taking time to rest and recharge not only allows the body to recover but also promotes mental clarity, emotional stability, and overall resilience.

Restorative activities such as meditation, gentle yoga, or leisurely walks can further enhance the benefits of rest by promoting relaxation, reducing stress, and improving sleep quality. These activities help activate the parasympathetic nervous system, often referred to as the "rest and digest" system, which counteracts the effects of the sympathetic nervous system's "fight or flight" response triggered during intense exercise.

Moreover, incorporating rest days into your fitness routine can help prevent burnout and maintain long-term adherence to your training program. By listening to your body's signals and honoring its need for rest, you can strike a balance between challenging workouts and adequate recovery, ultimately supporting your overall fitness goals and well-being. Remember, rest is not a sign of weakness but a crucial component of a balanced and sustainable approach to fitness.

In the realm of fitness, mobility work often takes a back seat to more traditional forms of exercise like strength training and cardio. However, overlooking mobility can be a critical mistake, as it plays a foundational role in both injury prevention and overall performance enhancement.

Mobility refers to the ability of a joint or group of joints to move freely through a full range of motion. It encompasses flexibility, joint stability, and neuromuscular control, all of which are essential for optimal movement quality and efficiency. Without adequate mobility, movements become restricted, inefficient, and prone to injury.

Incorporating mobility exercises into your fitness routine can yield a multitude of benefits. First and foremost, mobility work helps to improve flexibility, allowing muscles and joints to move more freely without restrictions.

This increased flexibility not only enhances performance in physical activities but also reduces the risk of strain or injury during exercise.

Moreover, mobility work targets joint stability, which is crucial for maintaining proper alignment and reducing the risk of overuse injuries. By strengthening the muscles surrounding a joint and improving neuromuscular control, mobility exercises help to create a stable foundation from which to move, jump, and lift with greater control and precision.

Dynamic stretches, foam rolling, and mobility drills are just a few examples of effective mobility exercises that can be incorporated into your routine. Dynamic stretches involve moving through a full range of motion in a controlled manner, helping to improve flexibility and prepare the body for activity. Foam rolling, on the other hand, utilizes self-myofascial release techniques to alleviate muscle tension and improve tissue quality. Mobility drills target specific muscle groups or movement patterns, helping to address areas of stiffness or weakness and improve overall movement efficiency.

In addition to enhancing physical performance, mobility work can also play a crucial role in injury rehabilitation and recovery. By addressing areas of tightness or weakness, mobility exercises can help to alleviate pain, improve joint function, and restore normal movement patterns following injury or overuse.

Ultimately, prioritizing mobility work in your fitness routine is essential for maintaining optimal movement quality, reducing the risk of injury, and maximizing performance potential. Whether you're an athlete looking to improve athletic performance or a recreational exerciser seeking to enhance overall well-being, incorporating regular mobility exercises can help you move better, feel better, and perform better in all aspects of life. Remember, mobility is the foundation upon which all movement is built, so invest in your mobility today for a healthier, more resilient body tomorrow.

Massage therapy is not just a luxury; it's an integral component of any comprehensive rest and recovery regimen. Whether you're an athlete pushing your limits in the gym or someone dealing with the stresses of everyday life, incorporating massages and deep pressure point release techniques into your routine can provide a myriad of benefits for both physical and mental well-being.

Professional massages offer more than just relaxation—they are a powerful tool for promoting recovery and enhancing overall performance. One of the primary benefits of massage therapy is its ability to improve blood circulation. By applying gentle pressure to the muscles and soft tissues, massages help to increase blood flow, delivering oxygen and essential nutrients to the muscles while flushing out metabolic waste products. This improved circulation not only accelerates the healing process but also helps to reduce inflammation and alleviate soreness following intense workouts or periods of physical exertion.

Moreover, massages can target specific areas of tension and discomfort, providing relief from muscle tightness and stiffness. Techniques such as deep pressure point release focus on applying sustained pressure to trigger points or "knots" in the muscles, helping to release tension and promote relaxation. By addressing these areas of tension, massages can improve flexibility, range of motion, and overall mobility, making it easier to move and perform daily activities without discomfort or pain.

Beyond the physical benefits, massages also offer significant mental and emotional benefits. The gentle touch and soothing strokes of a massage therapist can promote relaxation, reduce stress levels, and improve mood. Additionally, massage therapy has been shown to stimulate the release of endorphins—natural pain-relieving and mood-boosting hormones—further enhancing feelings of well-being and relaxation.

Incorporating massages and deep pressure point release techniques into your rest and recovery routine can be a game-changer for your overall health and fitness. Whether you choose to book a session with a professional massage therapist or use self-massage tools such as foam rollers or massage balls at home, prioritizing regular massage therapy can help you recover faster, reduce the risk of injury, and optimize your performance both in and out of the gym.

Remember, self-care is not selfish—it's essential for maintaining balance, health, and vitality in the long run. So treat yourself to a massage and experience the transformative power of touch for yourself. Your body and mind will thank you for it.

Chiropractic care offers a holistic approach to wellness by focusing on the relationship between the spine and the nervous system. Through chiropractic adjustments, chiropractors aim to restore proper alignment to the spine, which can have far-reaching effects on overall health and well-being, including improved mobility, reduced pain, and enhanced performance.

One of the primary benefits of chiropractic care is its ability to address imbalances in the musculoskeletal system. Over time, poor posture, repetitive movements, and injuries can lead to misalignments in the spine, known as subluxations. These misalignments can interfere with the proper function of the nervous system, resulting in a range of symptoms, including pain, stiffness, and reduced mobility. By gently realigning the spine through chiropractic adjustments, chiropractors can help alleviate pressure on the nerves and restore optimal function to the body.

In addition to addressing specific areas of pain or discomfort, chiropractic care focuses on improving joint function and mobility. When the spine is misaligned, it can place undue stress on the surrounding joints, leading to stiffness and restricted movement. Chiropractic adjustments can help restore proper joint alignment and range of motion, allowing for smoother, more efficient movement during physical activities. This improved joint function not only reduces the risk of injury but also enhances overall performance in sports and other physical pursuits.

Furthermore, chiropractic care can play a crucial role in supporting long-term fitness success by promoting proper biomechanics and alignment. When the spine is properly aligned, it creates a solid foundation for movement, allowing for optimal muscle activation and coordination. This, in turn, can help prevent injuries, improve athletic performance, and support overall health and well-being.

Regular chiropractic care is not just for athletes or those experiencing pain—it's beneficial for people of all ages and fitness levels. Whether you're an elite athlete looking to optimize your performance or someone simply looking to improve your quality of life, chiropractic adjustments can be a valuable addition to your wellness routine. By addressing spinal misalignments and promoting proper biomechanics, chiropractic care can help you move better, feel better, and live better for years to come.

Incorporating chiropractic care into your rest and recovery routine can complement other wellness practices such as exercise, nutrition, and stress management, creating a comprehensive approach to health and fitness. Whether you visit a chiropractor regularly or seek out occasional adjustments as needed, prioritizing spinal health can have profound benefits for your overall well-being and longevity.

Epsom salt baths are a time-tested remedy for promoting relaxation and soothing sore muscles. The main component of Epsom salt, magnesium sulfate, plays a crucial role in various physiological processes within the body, making it a valuable addition to any recovery routine.

Magnesium is an essential mineral that plays a role in over 300 enzymatic reactions in the body, including muscle function, nerve transmission, and energy production. During exercise, magnesium levels can become depleted as the muscles work hard and sweat is lost. This depletion can contribute to muscle cramps, fatigue, and delayed onset muscle soreness (DOMS).

Soaking in an Epsom salt bath allows the body to absorb magnesium through the skin, replenishing depleted levels and promoting relaxation of the muscles. This can help alleviate muscle tension, reduce cramping, and ease soreness, making it an ideal recovery strategy after intense workouts or periods of physical exertion.

In addition to its muscle-relaxing properties, Epsom salt baths can also help reduce inflammation and promote overall recovery. Magnesium sulfate has been shown to have anti-inflammatory effects, which can help reduce swelling and discomfort associated with overexertion or injury. By soaking in an Epsom salt bath, you can support the body's natural healing processes and accelerate recovery from strenuous activity.

Furthermore, Epsom salt baths offer a therapeutic and rejuvenating experience for both the body and mind. The warm water and soothing aroma of the salts create a calming environment that can help reduce stress, promote relaxation, and improve overall well-being. Taking time to unwind in an Epsom salt bath can be a valuable self-care practice, allowing you to recharge both physically and mentally.

To maximize the benefits of an Epsom salt bath, it's recommended to dissolve 1-2 cups of Epsom salt in warm bath water and soak for 20-30 minutes. You can enhance the experience further by adding essential oils, such as lavender or eucalyptus, which have their own therapeutic properties and can enhance the relaxation effects of the bath.

Incorporating Epsom salt baths into your regular routine can be a simple yet effective way to support your body's recovery process and promote overall well-being. Whether you're an athlete training for competition or someone simply looking to unwind after a long day, taking time for a relaxing soak can have profound benefits for your physical and mental health.

Proper nutrition and hydration are foundational elements of effective recovery strategies for athletes and fitness enthusiasts alike. Providing the body with the right nutrients and fluids is essential for facilitating muscle repair, replenishing energy stores, and supporting overall recovery processes.

A balanced diet comprising a variety of nutrient-dense foods is key to promoting optimal recovery. Lean proteins, such as chicken, fish, tofu, and legumes, are rich in essential amino acids necessary for muscle repair and growth. Incorporating these protein sources into post-workout meals and snacks can help support muscle recovery and adaptation.

Healthy fats, found in foods like avocados, nuts, seeds, and olive oil, are essential for hormone production, joint health, and overall cellular function. Including these fats in your diet can help reduce inflammation and support recovery processes.

Complex carbohydrates, such as whole grains, fruits, vegetables, and legumes, are the body's primary source of energy, especially during intense exercise. Consuming carbohydrates before and after workouts can help replenish glycogen stores and provide the energy needed for optimal performance and recovery.

In addition to macronutrients, micronutrients such as vitamins and minerals are also crucial for supporting recovery. These nutrients play important roles in various physiological processes, including energy metabolism, immune function, and tissue repair. Consuming a diverse array of fruits, vegetables, whole grains, and other nutrient-rich foods can help ensure that you're meeting your micronutrient needs and supporting overall recovery and well-being.

Hydration is equally important for supporting recovery processes, as water is essential for maintaining proper cellular function, regulating body temperature, and transporting nutrients throughout the body. Dehydration can impair physical performance and hinder recovery efforts, so it's essential to drink an adequate amount of water throughout the day, especially before, during, and after exercise.

Incorporating electrolyte-rich fluids, such as sports drinks or coconut water, can be beneficial for replacing electrolytes lost through sweat during intense exercise sessions. These fluids can help maintain proper hydration levels and support optimal recovery.

Overall, prioritizing proper nutrition and hydration is essential for supporting recovery, enhancing performance, and achieving long-term fitness success. By fueling your body with the right nutrients and fluids, you can optimize your body's ability to repair, rebuild, and adapt to the demands of your training regimen, ultimately leading to improved athletic performance and overall well-being.

Quality sleep is often referred to as the unsung hero of recovery, playing a pivotal role in promoting physical and mental well-being. While many focus on nutrition and exercise, the significance of sleep should not be underestimated in the pursuit of fitness success.

During sleep, the body enters various stages of restorative rest, facilitating essential processes crucial for recovery and overall health. One of these processes is muscle repair and growth, which occurs primarily during deep sleep stages.

Growth hormone secretion peaks during deep sleep, promoting protein synthesis and muscle recovery from the micro-tears incurred during exercise.

Moreover, sleep is essential for tissue repair and regeneration throughout the body. It allows for the repair of damaged cells and tissues, including those in muscles, tendons, and ligaments. Adequate sleep also supports immune function, helping the body fight off infections and recover from illness or injury more effectively.

In addition to physical recovery, sleep plays a crucial role in cognitive function and mental well-being. It enhances memory consolidation, learning, and decision-making processes, which are vital for skill acquisition and performance improvement in athletic endeavors. Furthermore, adequate sleep is associated with improved mood, reduced stress levels, and enhanced mental resilience, all of which contribute to overall fitness success.

To optimize sleep quality and duration, it's essential to prioritize good sleep hygiene practices. This includes maintaining a consistent sleep schedule, creating a relaxing bedtime routine, and optimizing sleep environment conditions, such as keeping the bedroom dark, quiet, and cool.

Limiting exposure to electronic devices and stimulating activities before bedtime can also promote better sleep quality by reducing the impact of blue light exposure and mental arousal. Instead, engage in calming activities such as reading, gentle stretching, or practicing relaxation techniques like deep breathing or meditation to prepare the body and mind for sleep.

While individual sleep needs may vary, aiming for seven to nine hours of quality sleep per night is generally recommended for adults to support optimal recovery and physical performance. By prioritizing sleep as an integral part of your fitness regimen, you can maximize the benefits of your training efforts, improve overall health and well-being, and enhance your long-term fitness success.

Stretching is a fundamental component of any well-rounded fitness program, offering numerous benefits for both physical performance and overall well-being. By incorporating stretching exercises into your routine, you can enhance flexibility, reduce muscle tension, and improve joint mobility, ultimately supporting optimal movement and reducing the risk of injury.

One of the primary benefits of stretching is its ability to improve flexibility and range of motion in the muscles and joints. Regular stretching helps elongate muscle fibers, making them more pliable and less prone to tightness and stiffness. This increased flexibility allows for greater freedom of movement during exercise and everyday activities, improving overall mobility and agility.

Moreover, stretching can help alleviate muscle tension and discomfort by promoting relaxation and reducing stress levels in the body. Stretching exercises encourage the release of endorphins, neurotransmitters that promote feelings of well-being and relaxation, helping to alleviate physical and mental tension accumulated throughout the day.

Incorporating stretching into your routine can also enhance muscular balance and symmetry, reducing the risk of muscle imbalances and postural abnormalities that can lead to injury. By targeting specific muscle groups through stretching exercises, you can address areas of tightness or weakness and promote more balanced muscle development throughout the body.

Stretching can be performed in various ways, including static stretching, dynamic stretching, and proprioceptive neuromuscular facilitation (PNF) stretching. Static stretching involves holding a stretch position for a set duration, typically 15-30 seconds, to lengthen the muscles gradually. Dynamic stretching involves moving through a range of motion in a controlled manner, warming up the muscles and preparing them for activity. PNF stretching combines passive stretching with muscle contraction to enhance flexibility and improve muscle activation.

Incorporate stretching exercises into your routine as part of a warm-up or cool-down routine, or perform them as standalone activities throughout the day to promote relaxation and flexibility. Focus on stretching major muscle groups, including the hamstrings, quadriceps, calves, hips, shoulders, and chest, and hold each stretch for 15-30 seconds to allow the muscles to relax and lengthen gradually.

By making stretching a regular part of your fitness regimen, you can improve flexibility, reduce muscle tension, and enhance overall mobility and performance, ultimately supporting long-term fitness success and well-being.

In the journey towards achieving fitness goals, it's crucial to understand that true progress is not solely measured by the intensity of workouts, but also by the quality of recovery. Rest and recovery play a vital role in allowing the body to adapt to physical stressors, repair damaged tissues, and rebuild stronger than before. By prioritizing restorative practices such as mobility work, massages, chiropractic care, Epsom salt baths, proper nutrition and hydration, sleep, and stretching, you can optimize your body's ability to recover and thrive over the long term.

Mobility work is essential for maintaining optimal joint function and preventing injuries. By incorporating mobility exercises into your routine, you can improve flexibility, range of motion, and joint stability, enhancing overall movement quality and performance. These exercises target specific muscle groups and movement patterns, helping to address imbalances and weaknesses that may lead to injury.

Professional massages and deep pressure point release techniques are powerful tools for promoting recovery and reducing muscle tension. Massage therapy improves blood circulation, reduces inflammation, and alleviates soreness, while deep pressure point release targets specific areas of tension, promoting relaxation and enhancing overall recovery.

Chiropractic care focuses on optimizing spinal alignment and joint function, which is essential for maintaining mobility and reducing the risk of injury. Regular chiropractic adjustments can address musculoskeletal imbalances, alleviate pain, and improve overall movement quality, supporting long-term fitness success.

Epsom salt baths offer a soothing and therapeutic way to promote recovery after intense workouts. Rich in magnesium sulfate, Epsom salt helps relax muscles, reduce inflammation, and relieve soreness, providing a natural and effective way to support recovery.

Proper nutrition and hydration are essential for supporting the body's recovery processes. Consuming a balanced diet rich in nutrients and staying hydrated ensures that your body has the fuel it needs to repair and rebuild muscle tissue, replenish energy stores, and support overall recovery.

Quality sleep is paramount for recovery and overall health. During sleep, the body undergoes essential repair and regeneration processes, including muscle growth and tissue repair. Aim for seven to nine hours of quality sleep per night to support optimal recovery and physical performance.

Stretching exercises help improve flexibility, reduce muscle stiffness, and prevent injuries by promoting relaxation and improving range of motion. Incorporate stretching into your routine as part of a warm-up or cool-down routine to support recovery and enhance overall mobility and performance.

In conclusion, recognizing the importance of rest and recovery is essential for achieving long-term fitness success. By integrating restorative practices into your routine, you can optimize your body's ability to recover and thrive, ultimately supporting your fitness goals and overall well-being. Remember, "Recovery is the New Workout," and prioritizing recovery strategies will help you achieve lasting success on your fitness journey.

NOTES:

CHAPTER 15

ALKA SHARMA

PLANNING AND PRESERVING WEALTH FOR GENERATIONS AND SETTING FUTURE GOALS FOR REAL ESTATE WEALTH CREATION

Estate planning involves meticulous organization, both for the present and the future, with the aim of creating a lasting family legacy. It's a comprehensive process that goes beyond simply distributing assets—it encompasses strategies to protect your wealth, minimize taxes, and ensure your wishes are carried out after you're gone.

At its core, estate planning is about safeguarding your assets and ensuring they are transferred to your chosen beneficiaries in the most efficient and effective manner possible. This often involves drafting legal documents such as wills, trusts, and powers of attorney to outline your wishes and designate individuals to manage your affairs in the event of incapacity.

But estate planning is not just about financial matters. It also involves decisions about healthcare directives, guardianship for minor children, and even charitable giving. By addressing these issues proactively, you can provide clarity and peace of mind for yourself and your loved ones, knowing that your affairs are in order and your legacy is protected.

Moreover, estate planning allows you to establish a framework for passing down not just your assets, but also your values, beliefs, and aspirations to future generations. Through careful planning and thoughtful decision-making, you can create a lasting impact that extends far beyond your lifetime, leaving behind a meaningful legacy that reflects your values and priorities.

Estate planning is the process of safeguarding your assets by implementing a strategic roadmap that outlines what actions will be taken and what will be avoided. Through thorough research and examination, it becomes evident that two well-known families, the Rockefellers and the Vanderbilts, provide instructive examples of effective estate planning.

For instance, the Rockefellers established a trust—an entity that restricts access to assets by heirs. In other words, a trust acts as a safeguard, placing a lock on assets to ensure they are managed responsibly and protected from potential misuse or mismanagement. This approach is crafted in the best interest of the family's long-term financial security and stability.

Conversely, the Vanderbilt family, once the wealthiest family of their time, serves as a cautionary tale. Their failure to implement effective estate planning strategies led to the dissipation of their wealth over subsequent generations. Without proper safeguards in place, assets may be vulnerable to various risks, including mismanagement, excessive taxation, and legal disputes.

These examples underscore the importance of estate planning in preserving and protecting wealth for future generations. By establishing trusts, wills, and other legal mechanisms, individuals can ensure their assets are managed prudently and in accordance with their wishes. Estate planning is not merely about wealth preservation—it's about creating a legacy that endures, providing for loved ones, and leaving a lasting impact for generations to come.

Two or three generations down the line, one sibling from a family worth billions has amassed considerable wealth, while not a single millionaire remains in the family. How did they transition from being the wealthiest family to having no substantial wealth at all? Individuals like Anderson Cooper may still be millionaires, but the broader family wealth has dissipated.

In contrast, the Rockefellers continue to thrive today, supporting their families and engaging in philanthropic endeavors that showcase the values passed down to their children. However, statistics show that a significant percentage of affluent families fail to sustain their wealth over multiple generations. Seventy percent of wealthy families lose their wealth by the second generation, and a staggering 90% lose it all by the third generation.

This underscores the importance of having a solid plan in place to preserve generational wealth. Even if you amass a fortune during your lifetime, without careful planning and consideration for future generations, that wealth can quickly vanish. Building generational wealth requires more than just accumulating money—it requires strategic planning and a clear vision for passing on assets, values, and opportunities to your children and grandchildren.

- Buy land: To understand generational wealth, it's essential to distinguish between personal wealth and family wealth. Personal wealth allows for discretionary use, such as having $100,000 in the bank. However, family wealth involves purchasing land, which is illiquid and challenging to convert to cash. Land tends to increase in demand over time, making it a valuable asset to pass down to future generations. By investing in land and having your children hold onto it, you can ensure its value continues to grow.

- Cash flow properties: Another strategy is investing in cash flow properties such as apartments, rentals, or hotels. These properties can be purchased and held onto, rather than sold, as your children become adults. Teaching them the golden rule of investing, they may start acquiring their own properties, gradually building a portfolio of passive income for the family.

- Build an evergreen business: Establishing a business that can withstand the test of time is crucial for generational wealth. Examples of such businesses include Hilton, Mercedes Benz, Ferrari, Louis Vuitton, and Chanel. These brands represent someone's legacy, structured to survive and thrive as a family business. Consider what business you can start that your children can be part of, carrying on the legacy for future generations.

Fun fact: Imagine your last name as a brand and envision what business you could start that your children will inherit and carry on for you. Allowing your children to flourish and eventually take over the business can lead to even greater success than you achieved. Research shows that 30% of family businesses are passed down to the second generation, and many millionaires are first-generation entrepreneurs who started from humble beginnings.

- Plan for the inevitable: While it may sound morbid, it's a fact that we will all pass away at some point. Ideally, you want to leave your wealth to your kids and grandkids. However, the state may impose inheritance taxes, also known as estate taxes, on the property of the deceased. In the UK, this tax is around 40%. Proper estate planning is essential to mitigate these taxes and ensure your wealth passes smoothly to your heirs, rather than being claimed by the state.

When building generational wealth, it's crucial to adhere to tax regulations and employ strategies to minimize taxes. Your tax advisor will provide guidance in understanding tax rules to ensure you don't pay more taxes than necessary. Wealthy individuals often pay minimal or no taxes by utilizing effective tax planning strategies.

It's crucial to recognize that no matter how much money your children may inherit, they should never cease earning. As the saying goes, "A person who can't earn for themselves can't hold onto wealth." This underscores the importance of instilling in them the principles of building and maintaining wealth. But how does one ensure that wealth endures over the long run?

One strategy is to hire an accountant who can help deduct expenses, especially business-related ones. Involving children in the family business can also be highly beneficial. By paying them for their intellectual property rights—such as ideas for tangible products like novels or textbooks—you not only compensate them but also nurture their entrepreneurial spirit and financial literacy. This approach ensures that they actively contribute to the family's wealth-building efforts while learning valuable lessons about responsibility and financial management.

I've observed numerous families where inherited wealth has led to undesirable outcomes. Many recipients of money or inheritances become obnoxious or irresponsible with their finances. Therefore, if your children don't start off on the right foot, it reflects a failure on the part of the parent, whether intentional or unintentional. Ultimately, it boils down to instilling the right values in your children from an early age. By teaching them the importance of responsibility, humility, and wise financial management, you can help ensure that they use their wealth responsibly and contribute positively to society.

Setting up a trust provides crucial protection, and wealthy individuals understand the importance of establishing legal entities to safeguard their wealth. By structuring trusts effectively, they can prevent their hard-earned assets from being squandered by their children.

A trust is a legal document that designates you as the guarantor, beneficiary, and trustee during your lifetime. In the event of any unforeseen circumstances or death, provisions are in place to ensure the smooth transition of assets. For example, if a spouse passes away, the surviving spouse typically assumes control of the trust. If both spouses are deceased, the trust is securely locked for the benefit of descendants. Families must develop a comprehensive plan to support their children and descendants, with guidelines in place to protect assets.

When setting up a trust, it's essential to ensure that your wishes are protected both during your lifetime and after your passing. Rich individuals utilize trusts as legal mechanisms to preserve their wealth and distribute it under specific circumstances. These structures can prevent children from depleting the family's hard-earned assets. Trusts also offer tax advantages, as they are taxed at lower rates and can be passed on to beneficiaries after the individual's death.

Protecting your estate requires careful planning, as it represents your legacy and personal fortune for future generations. Two main distinctions should be noted when considering trust setups.

Control, not ownership:

In essence, you don't necessarily need to own assets outright to have control over them in estate planning. For instance, if the estate is solely in your name, you could be subject to various taxes imposed by the government, such as transfer taxes and estate taxes. It's crucial to check with the city or state where you reside to avoid paying excessive taxes. Increased taxation can significantly diminish the value of the estate, a scenario commonly known as inheritance tax. It's important to be aware of the severity of these taxes to avoid any unpleasant surprises upon the owner's passing. For instance, my father passed away unexpectedly in the UK in 2021, and now my brother is facing a hefty 40% inheritance tax.

There are strategies to mitigate these taxes, such as placing assets into a charitable entity or family foundation. By doing so, the assets are no longer subject to taxes and are placed into a different realm. Many people have their children serve on the board of such entities, allowing them to continue receiving compensation.

Understanding the importance of a trust fund is paramount, as it offers protection that is not applicable to executors. If you do not own assets, your ex cannot claim them. Wealthy individuals embrace this concept, recognizing that control is often more valuable than ownership.

Successful multi-generational families understand the drawbacks of outright ownership. For example, if I were to give my son 100% ownership of the estate, he could be vulnerable in the event of a major auto accident or medical ailment resulting in substantial medical bills. By not owning assets outright, governments cannot lay claim to a portion of the money. Entrusting assets to heirs for safekeeping provides an added layer of protection.

Control holds more significance than ownership in estate planning. It's crucial to plan for known eventualities, such as the death of the owner, as well as unforeseen circumstances like the need for long-term care assistance as we age. Proper preparation ensures peace of mind and financial security for the future.

Ensure the estate is shielded from creditors in case of unforeseen events.

Maintain organized paperwork to facilitate smooth transfer and avoid probate proceedings. Probate, the process of validating the authenticity of a last will and testament, is part of estate planning administration.

Whenever possible, aim to avoid court involvement in probating the estate. It can be costly and results in public disclosure of estate affairs, which may not be desirable. Establishing entities can provide access to information for descendants or children while preserving privacy.

Successful multi-generational families understand that simply transferring ownership of assets to their children may not be the best approach. For instance, consider the scenario where I hypothetically gave 100% of my estate to my daughter. If she were to experience a major auto accident or significant medical ailments resulting in substantial bills, not owning the estate would safeguard it from government claims. In such a case, it would be safer to have heirs take over the estate.

Liabilities pose a significant risk to one's assets, and it's essential to understand how to protect them in the future. Consider the following example:

Imagine two investors—one in the stock market and the other in real estate. The stock market investor typically has fewer liabilities compared to the real estate investor. Real estate investments often come with associated liabilities, such as property taxes, mortgage payments, and potential legal issues.

Now, let's delve deeper into the real-world scenario of a person driving a vehicle who accidentally hits a pedestrian. If the pedestrian is a high-income earner, earning, say, $1 million per year, and tragically dies at the scene of the accident, their family may bring forth a massive lawsuit against the driver.

It's worth noting that insurance may not fully cover such a catastrophic event. Although such cases are rare, they do occur. In such instances, the other party may pursue legal action against wealthier families, seeking compensation beyond insurance coverage. As a result, the entire estate could be at risk of being wiped out in the event of a substantial lawsuit.

This example underscores the importance of asset protection strategies, such as liability insurance, trusts, and legal entities, to safeguard wealth and minimize the risk of financial devastation in unforeseen circumstances.

Estate planning should be a top priority, especially when considering how to protect assets. One effective strategy is consolidating assets under a single umbrella, such as an LLC (Limited Liability Company), particularly for real estate holdings. By having the LLC own all real estate assets, you create a centralized structure that simplifies management. In the event of your passing, your spouse can easily oversee the transfer of assets. Similarly, if your spouse faces medical challenges, control can smoothly transition to new trustees.

It's important to highlight the concept of a disregarded LLC, which typically means it's not subject to taxation. From a tax perspective, if assets are held under your name and someone brings legal action against you, those assets cannot be easily liquidated. This means that properties or assets cannot be readily converted into cash.

Once established, this structure becomes irrevocable after your passing. Therefore, it's crucial to carefully plan and execute these arrangements to safeguard your estate at all costs.

In cases of mixed marriages, where one or both spouses have children from previous relationships, establishing a living trust becomes even more crucial. A living trust allows you to specify exactly how you want your assets to be distributed after your passing, ensuring that your children from previous marriages are not unintentionally disinherited.

Without a clear estate plan in place, there's a risk that your assets could end up being distributed according to state intestacy laws, which may not align with your wishes. This can lead to complicated legal battles and potential estrangement among family members.

By setting up a living trust, you can designate specific assets to go to your children from previous marriages while also providing for your current spouse. This helps to avoid misunderstandings and conflicts among family members, ensuring that everyone is provided for according to your wishes. Additionally, a living trust offers privacy and avoids the probate process, allowing for a smoother and more efficient transfer of assets to your beneficiaries.

In the event of potential incapacitation, it's essential to have a plan in place. This often involves setting up a living trust. If you don't have a will, it's advisable to consult with a lawyer to prepare one. In my case, I met with my lawyer and drafted a will, ensuring that my assets will pass down to my children in the event of my passing.

Furthermore, it's important to understand the distinction between a will and a living trust. While a will outlines how your assets should be distributed after your passing, a living trust appoints a trustee to manage your estate should something happen to you. The trustee becomes the sole beneficiary of the estate held in the living trust.

Planning for the future involves more than just creating a will. It's about implementing a multi-generational strategy to protect your assets. By having a will in place, you can ensure that your wishes are carried out, and your assets are protected for future generations. It's also crucial to instill good values in your children, as they may play a role in managing and distributing your assets according to your wishes outlined in the will. Ultimately, having a will in place simplifies the transfer of assets and ensures a smooth flow of finances.

The question of whether to pass on your wealth directly to your children or grandchildren or to encourage them to build their own destiny and wealth is a thought-provoking one that touches on deep-rooted values and beliefs about wealth, success, and personal responsibility.

On one hand, providing an inheritance can offer your descendants financial security and opportunities that they might not otherwise have had. It can help them achieve their goals, pursue higher education, start businesses, or simply live comfortably without financial stress. Inheritance can also be seen as a form of support and love, allowing your family to benefit from the fruits of your labor and success.

On the other hand, there's the perspective of fostering independence and self-reliance. By encouraging your children or grandchildren to carve out their own paths and build their own wealth, you empower them to develop their skills, pursue their passions, and take ownership of their lives. This approach emphasizes the value of hard work, resilience, and personal achievement, instilling in them a sense of pride and accomplishment that comes from earning their own success.

Ultimately, the decision may depend on your values, beliefs, and goals for your family. Some may choose to provide a financial safety net for their loved ones, while others may prioritize the importance of self-reliance and personal growth. It's essential to consider both perspectives and weigh the potential impacts on your family's future well-being and fulfillment.

In closing, when considering your legacy, it's crucial to develop a concrete and systematic plan that will safeguard your estate and assets for generations to come.

Having clear, written instructions detailing who can access the funds and under what circumstances is essential. For instance, in a trust, it's wise to establish guidelines limiting withdrawals to no more than 5% annually. This principle, known as the '5% rule,' ensures responsible management of trust assets over time.

Moreover, a living trust can include provisions that reflect your values and aspirations for your beneficiaries. For example, you may specify that funds be used to support their travel, charitable endeavors, or personal development. By providing such directives, you empower the trustee to fulfill these wishes and enrich the lives of your loved ones according to your vision.

Legacy:

Creating a legacy plan entails understanding what you're planning for. If you prioritize education for your children, ensure there are funds available for their college tuition at the institutions of your choice. Trustees can oversee how these funds are allocated according to your wishes.

Life insurance plays a crucial role in funding your estate. Having permanent life insurance provides tax-free access to cash, which can be used for retirement purposes. This tax-free benefit extends into your retirement years, providing financial security. Additionally, life insurance can serve as a safety net in cases of disability or medical needs, alleviating the need to sell off assets. For instance, if you contribute to a foundation, it can offer tax savings for your family, ensuring your estate remains protected even after your passing.

NOTES:

CHAPTER 16

JENNIFER NICOLE LEE

LIFELONG WELLNESS: EMBRACING HEALTH AND WEALTH FOR A FULFILLING LIFE

By embracing a lifestyle that prioritizes both health and wealth, you can achieve a sense of fulfillment and abundance that transcends material possessions.

The holistic approach to wellness emphasizes the interconnectedness of physical, mental, and financial well-being, recognizing that these aspects of our lives are deeply intertwined and influence one another. Let's delve deeper into each dimension:

Physical Health

Physical health encompasses more than just the absence of illness or disease. It involves nourishing our bodies with nutritious food, engaging in regular exercise, prioritizing sleep, and attending to our overall well-being. By adopting healthy habits and lifestyle choices, we can enhance our physical vitality, boost our immune system, and reduce the risk of chronic diseases such as heart disease, diabetes, and obesity. Moreover, physical activity releases endorphins, neurotransmitters that promote feelings of happiness and reduce stress, contributing to our overall well-being.

Mental Health

Mental health refers to our emotional, psychological, and social well-being. It encompasses our thoughts, feelings, and behaviors and influences how we cope with stress, navigate relationships, and handle life's challenges. Prioritizing mental health involves practicing self-care, seeking support when needed, and cultivating resilience and emotional intelligence. Strategies such as mindfulness meditation, therapy, journaling, and spending time in nature can help promote mental wellness and foster a positive outlook on life.

Financial Health

Financial health involves managing our finances effectively, budgeting, saving, investing, and planning for the future. Achieving financial stability provides a sense of security and peace of mind, allowing us to pursue our goals and aspirations without undue stress or worry. Moreover, financial wellness enables us to afford essential resources such as healthcare, education, and leisure activities that support our overall well-being. By cultivating good financial habits and making informed financial decisions, we can create a solid foundation for long-term financial security and prosperity.

Interconnectedness

These dimensions of wellness are interconnected and mutually reinforcing. For example, regular exercise not only improves physical health but also enhances mood and reduces stress, benefiting our mental well-being. Similarly, financial stability provides the means to access resources and opportunities that support physical and mental well-being. Conversely, stress related to financial struggles can adversely affect both physical and mental health outcomes. Recognizing these interconnections allows us to adopt a more comprehensive approach to wellness that addresses all aspects of our lives.

Embracing Holistic Wellness

By embracing a holistic approach to wellness, we acknowledge the importance of nurturing our physical, mental, and financial well-being in tandem. Instead of viewing wellness as a series of isolated goals or achievements, we strive to create a harmonious balance across all dimensions of our lives. This holistic perspective empowers us to cultivate resilience, vitality, and fulfillment, enabling us to lead healthier, happier, and more meaningful lives.

Physical fitness goes beyond just the aesthetic benefits of looking good; it's about nourishing your body from the inside out. When we prioritize physical health, we lay a solid foundation for lifelong wellness. Here's why physical fitness is so crucial:

Enhancing Overall Quality of Life

Regular exercise, balanced nutrition, and sufficient rest are the cornerstones of physical fitness. By incorporating these elements into our daily lives, we not only improve our physical well-being but also enhance our mental and emotional health. Exercise releases endorphins, the body's natural feel-good hormones, which can alleviate stress, boost mood, and promote relaxation. Additionally, proper nutrition provides the fuel our bodies need to function optimally, supporting everything from energy levels to immune function. Adequate rest is equally important, allowing our bodies to repair and regenerate, ensuring we wake up feeling refreshed and rejuvenated.

Finding Joy in Movement

As a fitness expert, I encourage you to explore various forms of physical activity to find what brings you joy and fulfillment. Whether it's practicing yoga in the morning, going for a run in the park, or dancing to your favorite music, the key is to make movement an enjoyable and sustainable part of your lifestyle. When you engage in activities that you genuinely love, exercise becomes something to look forward to rather than a chore to be endured. Not only does this make it easier to stick to your fitness routine, but it also infuses your life with a sense of vitality and excitement.

Aligning with Your Lifestyle

It's essential to choose physical activities that align with your lifestyle and preferences. Consider factors such as your schedule, interests, and fitness goals when selecting your workout routine. If you're someone who enjoys being outdoors, consider hiking, cycling, or swimming. If you prefer the camaraderie of group fitness classes, explore options like Zumba, spinning, or boot camp workouts. The key is to find activities that you look forward to and that fit seamlessly into your life, making it easier to maintain consistency over the long term.

Cultivating Sustainable Habits

Building a lifelong commitment to physical fitness requires cultivating sustainable habits that support your health and well-being. Start by setting realistic goals and creating a plan that allows for flexibility and adaptability. Focus on progress rather than perfection, celebrating your achievements along the way. Surround yourself with a supportive community of like-minded individuals who can cheer you on and hold you accountable. By prioritizing your physical fitness and making it a non-negotiable part of your lifestyle, you'll reap the rewards of improved health, vitality, and longevity for years to come.

Strategic Money Management

Financial fitness begins with strategic money management practices that allow us to effectively allocate our resources. This includes creating and sticking to a budget that outlines our income, expenses, and savings goals. By tracking our spending habits and identifying areas where we can cut back or save more, we can maximize our financial resources and work towards achieving our financial goals.

Building Wealth through Investing

Investing is a key aspect of financial fitness, as it allows us to grow our wealth over time. In "The Successful Path to Financial and Physical Fitness," we provide practical strategies for investing wisely, whether it's through stocks, bonds, real estate, or other investment vehicles. We emphasize the importance of diversification and risk management to ensure a balanced and resilient investment portfolio.

Planning for the Future

Retirement planning is another crucial component of financial fitness. By starting early and contributing regularly to retirement accounts such as 401(k)s or IRAs, we can build a nest egg that will support us in our golden years. We offer guidance on setting retirement goals, estimating retirement expenses, and creating a savings plan that aligns with our long-term financial objectives.

Empowering Financial Independence

Ultimately, financial fitness is about empowering ourselves to achieve financial independence and freedom. It's about having the resources and flexibility to pursue our passions, support our loved ones, and live life on our own terms. By implementing the strategies outlined in our book, readers can take control of their financial futures and create lasting prosperity for themselves and their families.

Embracing Abundance Mindset

Being coined "The Queen of Manifesting", I help my clients to remove blocks, stopping wealth, abundance and prosperity to enter into their lives. So in addition to practical financial strategies, we also encourage readers to cultivate an abundance mindset—a belief that there is more than enough wealth and opportunity to go around. By shifting our mindset from scarcity to abundance, we open ourselves up to new possibilities and attract prosperity into our lives. With the right mindset and the right tools, achieving financial fitness is not only possible but within reach for anyone committed to their financial well-being.

Health and Financial Success

Research consistently demonstrates that individuals who prioritize their health often reap financial rewards. This correlation arises from several key factors:

- Productivity and Performance: Physical fitness is closely linked to cognitive function, energy levels, and overall productivity. When we prioritize our health through regular exercise, proper nutrition, and adequate sleep, we enhance our ability to perform at our best in both personal and professional pursuits. This heightened productivity often translates into increased earning potential and career advancement opportunities.

- Healthcare Costs: Maintaining good health can significantly reduce healthcare expenses over the long term. By investing in preventive care and adopting healthy lifestyle habits, individuals can minimize the risk of chronic diseases and costly medical interventions. Lower healthcare costs contribute to greater financial stability and resilience.

- Quality of Life: Physical fitness enhances our overall quality of life, allowing us to enjoy greater vitality, mobility, and longevity. As a result, we are better positioned to pursue our goals, engage in meaningful activities, and seize opportunities for personal and professional growth. This holistic well-being contributes to a more fulfilling and satisfying life, which extends beyond financial success alone.

Financial Resources and Health

Conversely, financial success can also have a profound impact on our health and well-being. Individuals who achieve financial stability and abundance often experience several health-related benefits:

- Access to Healthcare: Financial resources enable individuals to access high-quality healthcare services, including preventive screenings, medical treatments, and wellness programs. Having adequate health insurance coverage and financial resources to cover out-of-pocket expenses can facilitate timely healthcare interventions and promote better health outcomes.

- Healthcare Affordability: Financial stability reduces the stress and financial burden associated with healthcare expenses. Individuals with ample financial resources are better equipped to afford necessary medical treatments, medications, and therapies without compromising their financial security or well-being.

- Lifestyle Choices: Financial success provides individuals with the means to make healthier lifestyle choices, such as joining fitness clubs, purchasing nutritious foods, and engaging in leisure activities that promote physical and mental well-being. Access to resources and opportunities can empower individuals to prioritize their health and adopt sustainable lifestyle habits that support long-term wellness.

Embracing Holistic Well-Being

In essence, the intersection of health and wealth underscores the importance of embracing holistic well-being. By recognizing the interconnectedness of physical fitness and financial success, individuals can cultivate a balanced approach to life that prioritizes both their health and financial goals. By investing in our health and wealth simultaneously, we can optimize our overall well-being and create a foundation for a fulfilling and prosperous life.

Health is Wealth: The Value of Well-being

Your health is your greatest asset, and investing in it pays dividends throughout your life. By prioritizing your physical and mental well-being, you set yourself up for greater productivity, creativity, and resilience in all areas of your life, including your finances.

Wealth Enables Wellness: The Power of Financial Freedom

Financial freedom provides the resources and flexibility to prioritize your health and well-being. When you have financial security, you can afford nutritious food, quality healthcare, and opportunities for personal growth and self-care. Moreover, financial independence frees you from the stress and constraints that can compromise your health and happiness.

Embracing a Lifestyle of Abundance

In closing, I invite you to embrace a lifestyle of abundance that celebrates both health and wealth. By nurturing your body, mind, and finances, you can create a fulfilling life that is rich in vitality, prosperity, and well-being.

As you embark on this journey toward lifelong wellness, remember that success is not measured solely by the size of your bank account or the number on the scale. True success lies in the balance and harmony you achieve between your physical, mental, and financial health.

Here's to a lifetime of vibrant health, abundant wealth, and boundless joy!

NOTES:

CHAPTER 17

ALKA SHARMA

HARNESSING THE POWER OF MINDFULNESS FOR FINANCIAL WELL-BEING

As someone deeply immersed in the realm of real estate investing and financial expertise, I've witnessed firsthand the transformative power that mindfulness can exert over one's financial trajectory. Now, let's delve into the depths of this synergy and uncover the secrets to achieving enduring wealth and abundance through mindfulness.

Mindfulness serves as a guiding beacon, illuminating the path to financial prosperity with clarity and intention. At its essence, mindfulness entails being fully present in the moment, with a heightened awareness of our thoughts, emotions, and actions. When applied to the realm of finance, mindfulness serves as a catalyst for profound shifts in mindset and behavior, paving the way for sustainable wealth accumulation and abundance.

One of the fundamental pillars of mindful finance lies in the cultivation of conscious spending habits. In our consumer-driven society, it's all too easy to succumb to impulsive purchases and frivolous expenditures, draining our financial resources in the process. However, through the practice of mindfulness, we gain a newfound awareness of our spending patterns and habits. By consciously examining each financial transaction and discerning whether it aligns with our values and long-term goals, we empower ourselves to make informed choices that contribute to our financial well-being.

Furthermore, mindfulness acts as a potent antidote to the pervasive stress and anxiety often associated with financial matters. The uncertainty of economic fluctuations and the pressures of financial responsibilities can weigh heavily on our minds, leading to feelings of overwhelm and apprehension. Yet, through mindfulness practices such as deep breathing, meditation, and visualization, we cultivate a sense of inner calm and resilience in the face of adversity. By anchoring ourselves in the present moment and releasing attachment to future outcomes, we liberate ourselves from the shackles of financial worry and embrace a state of profound peace and equanimity.

Moreover, mindfulness fosters a mindset of abundance and gratitude, transforming our relationship with money from one of scarcity to one of abundance. Rather than fixating on what we lack or yearning for more, we learn to appreciate and celebrate the blessings already present in our lives. Through gratitude practices and mindfulness exercises, we awaken to the inherent richness of our existence, transcending the narrow confines of material wealth and discovering boundless abundance in the present moment.

When it comes to real estate investing, mindfulness emerges as a guiding compass, informing our investment decisions with clarity and discernment. By attuning ourselves to the subtle nuances of the market and listening to our intuition, we navigate the complexities of real estate with grace and precision. Through mindful analysis and strategic planning, we identify lucrative opportunities and mitigate risks, ultimately propelling us towards greater financial success and fulfillment.

Mindfulness stands as a potent catalyst for achieving lasting wealth and abundance in our lives. By cultivating awareness, presence, and gratitude in our financial journey, we transcend the limitations of scarcity and embrace the infinite possibilities of abundance. As we embark on this transformative odyssey of mindful finance, may we harness the full potential of our inner wisdom and usher forth a new era of prosperity and fulfillment.

Mindfulness is a powerful practice that transcends the boundaries of time and space, anchoring us firmly in the present moment. At its core, mindfulness invites us to engage with life's experiences with heightened awareness and clarity, allowing us to fully savor the richness of each moment. When we extend this practice to the realm of finance, we unlock the potential for profound transformation in our relationship with money, spending, and investing.

Imagine approaching your financial decisions with a sense of calm, clarity, and intentionality. Rather than being driven by impulses or influenced by external pressures, you become the master of your financial destiny, empowered to make choices that resonate deeply with your long-term goals and aspirations. This is the essence of mindful finance.

By cultivating awareness and presence in our financial decisions, we liberate ourselves from the grip of reactive patterns and unconscious behaviors that often lead to financial hardship. Instead of mindlessly splurging on unnecessary purchases or succumbing to the allure of fleeting trends, we pause, breathe, and consciously evaluate the implications of our actions on our financial well-being.

Mindfulness allows us to discern between our needs and wants, prioritizing the fulfillment of our long-term goals over short-term gratification. It enables us to distinguish between essential expenses that contribute to our well-being and frivolous indulgences that detract from our financial stability. Through this discernment, we develop a sense of financial clarity and purpose, aligning our spending habits with our values and priorities.

It serves as a powerful antidote to the allure of instant gratification and the fear of missing out (FOMO) that often plague our financial decisions. By cultivating a sense of inner calm and groundedness, we resist the impulse to chase after fleeting pleasures or succumb to societal pressures to keep up with the Joneses. Instead, we cultivate patience, discipline, and resilience, knowing that true wealth is built over time through consistent, mindful actions.

Mindfulness empowers us to approach the markets with a sense of equanimity and discernment. Rather than being swayed by market fluctuations or succumbing to the fear of potential losses, we maintain a steady focus on our long-term investment objectives. Through mindful analysis and strategic planning, we identify opportunities that align with our financial goals and risk tolerance, while also being mindful of the inherent uncertainties of the market.

Mindfulness revolutionizes the way we approach money, spending, and investing, enabling us to break free from reactive patterns and make choices that honor our long-term well-being. As we cultivate awareness and presence in our financial decisions, we embark on a journey of empowerment, fulfillment, and lasting prosperity.

Becoming aware of your spending patterns is a crucial step in harnessing the transformative power of mindfulness for financial well-being. In today's consumer-driven culture, it's all too easy to fall into the trap of mindless spending, where purchases are driven by impulse or habit rather than conscious intention. However, by shining a light on our spending habits through the lens of mindfulness, we can break free from these automatic patterns and take control of our financial destiny.

Mindless spending not only drains our financial resources but also undermines our ability to achieve our long-term financial goals. Whether it's indulging in unnecessary purchases, succumbing to the allure of instant gratification, or mindlessly swiping our credit cards, these impulsive behaviors can chip away at our financial stability and hinder our progress towards financial freedom.

Through mindfulness techniques such as conscious spending exercises and tracking your expenses, we can gain invaluable insight into our financial habits and behaviors. Conscious spending exercises encourage us to pause and reflect before making a purchase, asking ourselves questions like: "Is this purchase aligned with my values and priorities?" "Will it bring me long-term satisfaction and fulfillment?" By cultivating this level of awareness, we can avoid succumbing to impulse buys and make choices that truly support our financial well-being.

Tracking your expenses is another powerful mindfulness practice that can shed light on where your money is going and identify areas for improvement. By diligently recording every expenditure, whether it's a cup of coffee or a major purchase, you gain clarity on your spending patterns and can identify areas where you may be overspending or allocating resources inefficiently. This heightened awareness empowers you to make conscious choices that align with your financial goals and priorities.

Moreover, mindfulness helps us cultivate a deeper understanding of the underlying motivations behind our spending habits. Are we seeking to fill a void or alleviate emotional discomfort through retail therapy? Are we succumbing to societal pressures or trying to keep up with unrealistic expectations? By bringing awareness to the root causes of our spending behaviors, we can address them more effectively and develop healthier coping mechanisms that don't involve financial excess.

By integrating mindfulness into our approach to spending, we cultivate a sense of empowerment and mastery over our financial lives. We no longer feel at the mercy of external influences or driven by unconscious impulses; instead, we become conscious stewards of our financial resources, making deliberate choices that support our long-term well-being and fulfillment. As we embrace the practice of mindful spending, we pave the way for greater financial stability, freedom, and abundance in our lives.

In today's fast-paced and uncertain world, financial stress can often feel like an unavoidable burden, weighing heavily on our minds and dampening our sense of well-being. However, mindfulness offers a powerful antidote to the anxiety and overwhelm that often accompany financial worries. By incorporating mindfulness techniques into our daily lives, we can cultivate a sense of calm, resilience, and empowerment in the face of financial challenges.

At the heart of mindfulness lies the practice of being fully present in the moment, free from the distractions of past regrets or future anxieties. When it comes to managing financial stress, this present-moment awareness serves as a potent ally, enabling us to anchor ourselves in the here and now rather than being consumed by worries about the future.

Mindfulness techniques such as deep breathing, meditation, and visualization provide invaluable tools for calming the mind and soothing the nervous system. Deep breathing exercises, for example, activate the body's relaxation response, helping to reduce stress hormones and induce a state of calmness and clarity. By taking slow, deliberate breaths and focusing on the sensations of each inhale and exhale, we can quiet the chatter of our minds and cultivate a sense of inner peace.

Meditation, another cornerstone of mindfulness practice, offers a sanctuary for stillness and introspection amidst the chaos of daily life. Through regular meditation sessions, we learn to observe our thoughts and emotions with detachment, allowing them to arise and pass away without becoming entangled in their grip. By cultivating this space of inner stillness, we develop greater resilience in the face of financial challenges, recognizing that our worth and well-being are not contingent upon external circumstances.

Visualization, a powerful technique used in mindfulness and manifestation practices, allows us to create mental images of our desired financial outcomes and goals. By vividly imagining ourselves achieving financial stability, abundance, and success, we tap into the power of our subconscious mind to manifest these realities into existence. Through regular visualization exercises, we reprogram our beliefs and attitudes towards money, cultivating a mindset of abundance and possibility.

By anchoring ourselves in the present moment through mindfulness practices, we can alleviate anxiety about the future and focus on taking positive action steps towards financial stability and well-being. Rather than being consumed by worries and fears, we approach our financial challenges with clarity, resilience, and confidence. As we cultivate a deeper sense of mindfulness in our financial lives, we unlock the power to transform stress into strength, fear into courage, and uncertainty into opportunity.

Mindfulness extends far beyond the realm of stress management; it encompasses a profound shift in perspective that can revolutionize our relationship with money and abundance. When we approach our finances from a mindset of scarcity, we perceive the world through a lens of limitation and lack. This scarcity mindset often manifests as feelings of stress, fear, and anxiety about not having enough to meet our needs or achieve our desires.

However, mindfulness offers a transformative alternative: the cultivation of abundance and gratitude in our financial lives. Rather than focusing on what we lack or yearning for more, we shift our attention towards appreciating and celebrating the blessings already present in our lives. This shift in perspective opens the door to a wealth of opportunities and possibilities, allowing us to attract greater abundance into our lives through the power of gratitude.

Gratitude exercises serve as a cornerstone of mindfulness practice, inviting us to consciously acknowledge and express gratitude for the abundance that surrounds us. Whether it's the roof over our heads, the food on our table, or the relationships that enrich our lives, there is always something to be grateful for. By taking time each day to reflect on the blessings in our lives, we cultivate a sense of appreciation and contentment that transcends material wealth.

By focusing on what we do have rather than what we lack, we shift our energetic vibration and attract more abundance into our lives. This principle, often referred to as the law of attraction, suggests that like attracts like; when we radiate gratitude and abundance, we naturally draw more of the same towards us. By embodying a mindset of abundance, we become magnetic to opportunities, resources, and blessings that align with our desires and intentions.

Practicing mindfulness in our financial lives also involves reframing our relationship with money from one of scarcity to one of abundance. Rather than viewing money as a finite resource to be hoarded and guarded, we see it as a flowing and abundant energy that is meant to be circulated and shared. This shift in perspective allows us to approach our finances with a sense of openness, generosity, and trust, knowing that there is always enough to meet our needs and fulfill our dreams.

Mindfulness invites us to recognize and appreciate the abundance that already exists within and around us. By practicing gratitude, shifting our mindset from scarcity to abundance, and embodying a spirit of generosity and trust, we open ourselves to a world of limitless possibilities and opportunities. As we cultivate mindfulness in our financial lives, we unlock the power to attract greater abundance, prosperity, and fulfillment into every aspect of our existence.

Mindfulness, with its capacity to deepen self-awareness and clarity of mind, serves as a potent ally in the realm of investment decision-making. Beyond its role in managing stress and cultivating abundance, mindfulness has the power to enhance our ability to make informed, strategic, and aligned investment choices that support our financial goals.

In the fast-paced world of investing, we are often bombarded with a cacophony of external influences—from market trends and economic forecasts to the opinions of financial experts and media pundits. This constant barrage of information can cloud our judgment and lead to impulsive or irrational decision-making. However, by cultivating mindfulness, we can learn to quiet the noise of external influences and tune into our inner wisdom and intuition.

Mindfulness invites us to step back from the frenetic energy of the market and cultivate a sense of inner calm and clarity. Through mindfulness practices such as meditation, deep breathing, and mindfulness-based stress reduction (MBSR) techniques, we develop the capacity to observe our thoughts, emotions, and impulses with detachment and non-judgment. This heightened self-awareness allows us to discern between external noise and internal guidance, empowering us to make decisions that are aligned with our values, goals, and risk tolerance.

By quieting the chatter of our minds and tuning into our intuition, we gain access to a deeper reservoir of wisdom and insight that transcends rational analysis alone. This intuitive intelligence, often referred to as gut instinct or inner knowing, arises from a place of deep inner knowing and interconnectedness with the greater intelligence of the universe. When we cultivate mindfulness, we become attuned to this intuitive guidance, allowing it to inform our investment decisions with clarity and confidence.

Mindfulness enhances our ability to remain present and grounded in the midst of market volatility and uncertainty. Rather than being swept away by fear or greed, we maintain a steady focus on our long-term investment objectives and remain open to the ever-changing dynamics of the market. This adaptability and resilience enable us to navigate fluctuations with grace and poise, making adjustments to our investment strategies as needed while staying true to our overarching financial goals.

In essence, mindfulness serves as a guiding light in the realm of investment decision-making, illuminating the path to informed, aligned, and empowered choices. By quieting the noise of external influences and tuning into our inner wisdom and intuition, we unlock the power to make decisions that support our financial well-being and contribute to our long-term prosperity. As we cultivate mindfulness in our investment approach, we embark on a journey of greater clarity, confidence, and success in navigating the complexities of the financial markets.

In conclusion, mindfulness emerges as a cornerstone of achieving financial well-being and abundance, offering a transformative pathway to lasting prosperity. By cultivating awareness, presence, and gratitude in our financial lives, we unlock the keys to making empowered choices that align with our long-term goals and aspirations. Through practical exercises, insightful guidance, and dedicated practice, we can embark on a journey of mindful wealth and unlock the full potential of our financial future.

Cultivating awareness is the first step towards harnessing the power of mindfulness in our financial journey. By bringing conscious attention to our spending habits, investment decisions, and overall financial behaviors, we gain invaluable insight into the patterns and tendencies that shape our financial reality. Through this heightened awareness, we become empowered to identify areas for improvement, make necessary adjustments, and align our actions with our financial goals.

Presence is the foundation upon which mindful financial decision-making rests. By anchoring ourselves in the present moment, we release attachment to past regrets and future anxieties, allowing us to focus our energy and attention on the opportunities and challenges that lie before us. In the midst of market volatility and uncertainty, presence enables us to maintain a steady course, grounded in clarity and resilience. By cultivating presence, we cultivate the capacity to respond to financial circumstances with wisdom and discernment, rather than reacting from a place of fear or impulse.

Gratitude serves as a potent catalyst for inviting abundance into our financial lives. By shifting our focus from scarcity to abundance, we awaken to the myriad blessings that surround us each day—from the roof over our heads to the relationships that enrich our lives. Through gratitude practices such as journaling, reflection, and acts of kindness, we cultivate a deep sense of appreciation for the abundance that already exists within and around us. This attitude of gratitude opens the floodgates to greater blessings and opportunities, as we attract more of what we focus on into our lives.

Mindfulness offers a roadmap to mindful wealth—a journey of self-discovery, empowerment, and fulfillment in the realm of finance. By integrating mindfulness into our financial lives, we unlock the potential to make conscious, intentional choices that support our long-term prosperity and well-being. Through dedicated practice and a commitment to growth, we can embark on a journey of mindful wealth and unlock the full potential of our financial future.

NOTES:

CHAPTER 18

JENNIFER NICOLE LEE

CULTIVATING GRATITUDE FOR OPTIMAL HEALTH AND SUCCESS

In my final solo chapter of this book, as we draw the curtains on our journey towards holistic wellness and prosperity, I am compelled to shed light on the transformative force of gratitude. Gratitude isn't just a fleeting emotion; it's a dynamic energy that permeates every aspect of our being, transcending mere feelings of thankfulness to become a catalyst for profound change. From nurturing our physical well-being to shaping our financial success, gratitude holds the power to uplift and enrich every facet of our existence.

At its core, gratitude is a practice—a conscious choice to acknowledge and appreciate the abundance that surrounds us, even in the midst of challenges or adversity. It's about recognizing the countless blessings, both big and small, that grace our lives each day, and expressing genuine appreciation for them. This practice of gratitude isn't reserved for moments of celebration or abundance; it's equally important during times of struggle or uncertainty, serving as a guiding light that illuminates the path forward.

When we cultivate a mindset of gratitude, we shift our focus from what we lack to what we have, from scarcity to abundance. Rather than dwelling on perceived deficiencies or shortcomings, we become attuned to the myriad blessings that enrich our lives—the love of family and friends, the beauty of nature, the opportunities for growth and learning. This shift in perspective opens our hearts to receive the gifts that life has to offer, allowing us to experience greater joy, fulfillment, and contentment.

But the impact of gratitude extends beyond our emotional well-being; it also has tangible effects on our physical health. Research has shown that practicing gratitude can boost our immune system, lower our blood pressure, and reduce symptoms of depression and anxiety. By cultivating a grateful attitude, we not only enhance our psychological resilience but also promote overall health and well-being.

Gratitude serves as a powerful magnet for attracting abundance and prosperity into our lives. When we approach our financial goals with a spirit of gratitude, we shift our vibration to one of receptivity and abundance, opening ourselves up to receive the resources and opportunities that align with our desires. This isn't about wishful thinking or passive waiting; it's about taking inspired action from a place of gratitude and trust, knowing that the universe is conspiring in our favor.

It is more than just a virtue—it's a way of life, a lens through which we view the world and navigate our journey towards holistic wellness and prosperity. As we embrace the transformative power of gratitude, we awaken to the boundless possibilities that await us, and we step into a future filled with abundance, joy, and fulfillment. So, let us embark on this journey together and uncover the limitless potential of gratitude to enrich every aspect of our lives.

Gratitude isn't just a fleeting emotion or a polite gesture; it's a profound mindset shift that should be an essential component of everyone's wellness program. When we cultivate gratitude, we not only enhance our emotional well-being but also nourish our physical health and overall vitality.

Research has shown that practicing gratitude can have a myriad of positive effects on our health, both mentally and physically. By shifting our focus from what we lack to what we have, gratitude reduces stress levels, lowers blood pressure, and boosts immune function. It promotes a sense of calmness and relaxation, allowing us to better cope with life's challenges and setbacks.

A consistent expression of gratitude has been linked to improved sleep quality, enhanced resilience, and increased levels of happiness and life satisfaction. When we approach life with a grateful heart, we cultivate a positive outlook that permeates every aspect of our existence. This positive mindset not only fosters greater emotional resilience but also strengthens our relationships and social connections.

Incorporating gratitude into our daily lives is essential for maintaining optimal health and well-being. Just as we prioritize exercise, nutrition, and sleep as essential components of our wellness routine, so too should we prioritize gratitude. By consciously practicing gratitude, we nourish our minds, bodies, and spirits, fostering a sense of balance, harmony, and vitality.

So, let us embrace the transformative power of gratitude and make it a cornerstone of our essential wellness program. By cultivating gratitude, we elevate our energy levels, boost our mood, and amplify our achievements. Let us embark on this journey towards greater health, happiness, and fulfillment, one grateful moment at a time. Remember, working out and eating healthy isn't an "I have to", it's an "I get to"!

I've personally witnessed the profound impact that gratitude can have on our physical health. When we approach our fitness journey with a heart full of gratitude, it transforms our entire relationship with exercise. Instead of viewing physical activity as a burdensome task or a punishment for indulgences, we begin to see it as a sacred gift—an opportunity to honor and celebrate the remarkable capabilities of our bodies. Gratitude infuses our workouts with a sense of purpose and meaning, inspiring us to move with joy, vitality, and appreciation for all that our bodies enable us to do.

But the benefits of gratitude extend far beyond the realm of physical health; they ripple outwards, influencing every aspect of our lives, including our financial well-being. When we approach our finances with a mindset of gratitude, it shifts our perspective from scarcity to abundance. Rather than fixating on what we lack or feeling stressed about our financial situation, we choose to focus on the wealth of blessings that surround us each day—the opportunities, resources, and support systems that uplift and sustain us.

Practicing gratitude isn't merely about uttering words of thanks; it's about embodying a spirit of appreciation and abundance in every moment of our lives. One powerful way to cultivate gratitude is through daily gratitude practices, such as keeping a gratitude journal or engaging in mindful reflection. By dedicating a few moments each day to acknowledge and express gratitude for the blessings in our lives, we train our minds to seek out and amplify the positive, even amidst adversity.

These gratitude practices serve as a reminder that even in the midst of challenges or setbacks, there is always something to be thankful for. By consciously focusing on the abundance that surrounds us, we cultivate a sense of resilience, optimism, and inner peace that empowers us to navigate life's ups and downs with grace and fortitude. As we embrace gratitude as a way of life, we open ourselves up to a world of infinite possibilities, where joy, fulfillment, and abundance abound.

Engaging in acts of kindness and generosity towards others is another potent way to cultivate gratitude in our lives. When we extend a helping hand or offer support to those in need, we not only brighten their day but also enrich our own lives in profound ways. The practice of giving back serves as a powerful reminder of the abundance of love, compassion, and interconnectedness that exists in the world.

Volunteering our time to serve others is a deeply rewarding experience that fosters a sense of connection and purpose. Whether it's lending a hand at a local soup kitchen, participating in a community clean-up event, or volunteering with a nonprofit organization, these acts of service allow us to make a tangible difference in the lives of others while also deepening our own sense of gratitude and fulfillment. By witnessing the impact of our actions firsthand, we gain a deeper appreciation for the blessings in our own lives and the opportunity to contribute positively to the world around us.

Similarly, donating to charity or supporting causes that align with our values is another meaningful way to practice gratitude. By sharing our resources with those in need, we acknowledge our abundance and express gratitude for the blessings we've received. Whether it's making a financial contribution to a charitable organization, donating goods to a local shelter, or sponsoring a child's education, these acts of generosity remind us of the power we have to make a difference in the lives of others and the importance of giving back to our communities.

Even simple gestures of kindness, such as offering a smile, a listening ear, or a word of encouragement, can have a profound impact on those around us. These small acts of kindness not only brighten someone's day but also cultivate a sense of connection and compassion within ourselves. By taking the time to acknowledge and uplift others, we create a ripple effect of positivity and gratitude that extends far beyond the moment.

In essence, the practice of giving back is a powerful way to cultivate gratitude and enrich our lives. Whether through volunteering our time, donating to charity, or simply offering kindness and compassion to those around us, acts of generosity remind us of the abundance of love and goodness that exists in the world. As we extend kindness and support to others, we nourish our own spirits and deepen our appreciation for the blessings in our lives.

In conclusion, gratitude emerges as a powerful tool with the potential to enhance every facet of our lives, from our physical health to our financial success. By embracing gratitude as a guiding principle and integrating gratitude practices into our daily routines, we unlock the key to a more vibrant, fulfilling, and abundant existence.

Gratitude serves as a catalyst for transformation, elevating our energy levels and infusing our lives with a sense of vitality and joy. When we cultivate an attitude of gratitude, we shift our focus from what is lacking to what is present, from scarcity to abundance. This shift in perspective not only enhances our overall well-being but also empowers us to navigate life's challenges with resilience and grace.

Moreover, gratitude has a profound impact on our mental and emotional health, fostering a sense of optimism, contentment, and inner peace. By consciously acknowledging and appreciating the blessings in our lives, we cultivate a positive mindset that shapes our perception of the world around us. This positive outlook not only enhances our mood but also strengthens our relationships, fosters greater empathy and compassion, and promotes overall psychological well-being.

In the realm of financial success, gratitude serves as a magnet for abundance and prosperity. By approaching our financial goals with a spirit of gratitude, we open ourselves up to receive the wealth of opportunities and resources that surround us. Rather than succumbing to feelings of scarcity or lack, we choose to focus on the abundance that already exists within and around us, thereby attracting greater financial success and fulfillment into our lives.

By incorporating gratitude practices into our daily lives, such as keeping a gratitude journal, practicing mindfulness, or expressing appreciation to others, we cultivate a deeper sense of gratitude and abundance. These simple yet powerful practices not only enhance our well-being on a personal level but also contribute to the collective upliftment of humanity as a whole.

So, let us commit to cultivating an attitude of gratitude and watch as our health and success soar to new heights. As we embrace gratitude as a way of life, we tap into the limitless potential of the universe and create a reality filled with joy, abundance, and fulfillment.

NOTES:

BONUS CHAPTER

POSITIVE AFFIRMATIONS FOR THE WEALTHY AND HEALTHY!!

1. I am abundant in wealth and health.
2. I am attracting prosperity effortlessly.
3. I am grateful for the abundance in my life.
4. I am worthy of all the success coming my way.
5. I am financially free and secure.
6. I am in perfect health, both mentally and physically.
7. I am radiating positive energy and vitality.
8. I am aligned with the universe's abundance.
9. I am surrounded by opportunities to grow my wealth.
10. I am deserving of all the blessings in my life.
11. I am attracting wealth and health with every breath.

12. I am open to receiving infinite prosperity.
13. I am prosperous in all areas of my life.
14. I am achieving my financial goals effortlessly.
15. I am living a life of abundance and fulfillment.
16. I am grateful for my vibrant health and wealth.
17. I am constantly expanding my wealth consciousness.
18. I am attracting prosperity with every positive thought.
19. I am creating a life filled with wealth and health.
20. I am worthy of experiencing boundless wealth.
21. I am in perfect harmony with the flow of abundance.
22. I am grateful for the wealth and health that surrounds me.
23. I am attracting wealth with ease and joy.
24. I am open to receiving all the riches of the universe.
25. I am a magnet for financial abundance.
26. I am embracing my wealth and health journey with joy.
27. I am grateful for the abundance that flows into my life.

28. I am worthy of all the prosperity that comes my way.

29. I am blessed with unwavering health and abundance.

30. I am living a life filled with prosperity and vitality.

31. I am attracting wealth effortlessly and naturally.

32. I am deserving of all the richness life has to offer.

33. I am grateful for the wealth and health that fills my life.

34. I am aligning myself with the energy of abundance.

35. I am attracting wealth with every positive action I take.

36. I am surrounded by opportunities to grow my wealth exponentially.

37. I am grateful for the financial freedom that enriches my life.

38. I am open to receiving all the blessings the universe has in store for me.

39. I am worthy of experiencing boundless health and prosperity.

40. I am attracting wealth and abundance with every step I take.

41. I am grateful for the abundance of health and wealth in my life.

42. I am deserving of all the success and prosperity coming my way.

43. I am aligned with the energy of abundance and prosperity.

44. I am attracting wealth effortlessly and joyfully.

45. I am open to receiving all the abundance the universe has to offer.

46. I am worthy of all the blessings that flow into my life.

47. I am grateful for the wealth and health that surrounds me every day.

48. I am attracting prosperity with ease and grace.

49. I am living a life filled with abundance and vitality.

50. I am open to receiving infinite wealth and health.

Now write your own!

____

____

____

____

____

____

CONCLUSION AND CLOSING REMARKS

As we reach the culmination of "The Successful Path to Financial and Physical Fitness: Your Winning Wealth and Health Comprehensive Lifestyle Formula," we are reminded of the profound impact that our financial and physical well-being have on our lives. Throughout this journey, we have explored the synergies between health and wealth, uncovering the interconnectedness of these fundamental aspects of human existence.

From the foundations of physical fitness to the principles of financial prosperity, we have delved into practical strategies and insightful guidance aimed at empowering you to achieve holistic well-being. Together, we have navigated the pathways to lifelong wellness, embracing the importance of balance, discipline, and purpose in our pursuit of success.

Closing Remarks:

As co-authors, Alka Sharma and Jennifer Nicole Lee, we extend our heartfelt gratitude to each reader who has embarked on this transformative journey with us. May the wisdom shared within these pages serve as a beacon of inspiration and empowerment as you navigate the twists and turns of life's journey.

Remember, true success lies not only in the attainment of wealth or physical fitness but in the harmonious integration of these elements to create a life of abundance, vitality, and fulfillment. As you continue along your path, may you find joy in the pursuit of your goals, strength in the face of challenges, and fulfillment in the realization of your dreams.

With unwavering dedication and boundless optimism, we invite you to embrace "The Successful Path to Financial and Physical Fitness" as a roadmap to a life of prosperity, vitality, and well-being.

For more coaching, masterclasses, courses, live and in person events, please visit our websites at www.AlkaSharma.com and www.JenniferNicoleLee.com

Wishing you health, wealth, and happiness on your journey ahead.

Warm regards,
Alka Sharma and **Jennifer Nicole Lee**

Made in the USA
Columbia, SC
16 September 2024